Think Like the
BUDDHA

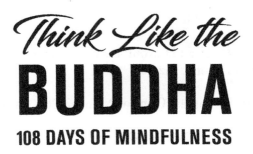

Think Like the BUDDHA
108 DAYS OF MINDFULNESS

VICTOR M. PARACHIN

HOHM PRESS
Chino Valley, Arizona

© 2020 Victor M. Parachin

All rights reserved. No part of this book may be reproduced in any manner without written permission from the publisher, except in the case of quotes used in critical articles and reviews.

Cover Design: Hohm Press

Interior Design and Layout: Becky Fulker, Kubera Book Design, Prescott, Arizona

Library of Congress Control Number: 2020940255

ISBN: 978-1-942493-61-7

Hohm Press
P.O. Box 4410
Chino Valley, AZ 86323
800-381-2700
http://www.hohmpress.com

This book was printed in the U.S.A. on recycled, acid-free paper using soy ink.

All wholesome words, deeds and thoughts have mindfulness as their root.—Buddha

Contents

Introduction	iv
The 108 Days	1
Index	215
Contact Information	220
About the Author	220
About Hohm Press	220

Introduction

During the year this book is published we experienced a seismic, global event due to the Covid-19 Pandemic. As a result, we have been delivered a powerful reminder about the importance of cultivating the ability to adapt and adjust to rapid change and challenge. It has become clearer and more imperative that dealing with the anxiety and fear forced upon us by a deadly virus involves deepening attention and awareness so that we are not overwhelmed by panic and hysteria. The enormous upheaval of this year should be heeded as a call to elevate mindfulness so that we move through this issue, and every other crisis, with a mind that is balanced, focused, stable, and grounded in wisdom.

The Buddha was the planet's most prominent practitioner and teacher of mindfulness.

Perhaps the most famous of all the stories about the Buddha is this one which took place shortly after his enlightenment. As the Buddha was walking along a path, he encountered a man with whom he exchanged simple greetings. The man noticed immediately that the stranger on the path exuded an extraordinary calm, confidence, serenity and stability. This led him to stop the Buddha and ask:

"My friend, are you a God?"

"No," said the Buddha.

The man continued: "Then are you a scholar of holy books?

Again, the Buddha answered no.

"Perhaps you are a priest, then, who is advanced in matters of ritual and chanting?"

Yet again, the Buddha smiled and said no.

"Then who are you, my friend?" the man finally asked.

The Buddha replied directly and concisely: "I am awake!"

Though that answer was an unusual way to define himself, the Buddha was speaking about mindfulness. Mindfulness simply means being alert, aware, attentive *moment by moment*. The simplest definition of mindfulness is *mental scrutiny*. When we have that mind skill, the result of our living is positive, as the Buddha noted: "All wholesome words, deeds and thoughts have mindfulness as their root." However, if the mind is not trained, the result of our living will have a negative shadow and the Buddha's statement could properly be re-phrased: "All unwholesome words, deeds and thoughts have mind*less*ness as their root."

The readings in this book offer gentle reminders to be mindful about our daily thoughts, words and actions because the opposite of mindfulness is forgetfulness and neglect. All too often we "forget" to be present. We neglect to be mindful when eating, listening, speaking, working, studying, seeing the sunrise and the sunset, being with friends or sipping a cup of tea. As a result, we fail to live our lives to their fullest potential and experience the joy of living.

This book, *Think Like the Buddha*, offers 108 days of mindfulness. The stories and lessons are brought together to provide insight, information, instruction and inspiration for the reader to cultivate daily mindfulness. To make the best use of the book and to gain the most benefit, I offer these suggestions:

Read one entry per day for the 108 days.

"Ritualize" your reading by doing it at the same time and same place daily.

After the reading, take three-to-five minutes to practice "digestion" meditation. Sit silently and reflect on how that day's reading can apply and appear in your life.

By reading in this more leisurely and intentional way, the practice of mindfulness will expand in your daily living. You will find yourself paying closer attention to thoughts, feelings, words, actions and experiences. And, in so doing, you will unleash your power to respond rather than react and to act intentionally rather than habitually.

—Victor M. Parachin

The 108 Days

DAY 1

Abandon and Cultivate

Happiness depends on properly cultivating what is wholesome and discarding what is unwholesome.
—Sonam Rinchen

Here's a simple yet foundational teaching from the Buddha:

> Abandon what is unskillful. One can abandon the unskillful. If it were not possible, I would not ask you to do so. If this abandoning of the unskillful would bring harm and suffering, I would not ask you to abandon it. But as the abandoning of the unskillful brings benefit and happiness, therefore, I say, "Abandon what is unskillful!"

Having read that, pause to ask yourself: "What's not working well in my life? What area is unskillful and no longer serves me well?" This could be anything from a job, a career, a relationship, an addiction, etc. Once identified, do what the Buddha advises: "Abandon what is unskillful" in order to experience more benefit and happiness.

There's a second part to the Buddha's teaching:

Cultivate that which is skillful. One can cultivate the skillful. If it were not possible, I would not ask you to do it. If this cultivation of the skillful would bring harm and suffering, I would not ask you to cultivate it. But as the cultivation of the skillful brings benefit and happiness, therefore, I say, "Cultivate that which is skillful!"

Now, having read this second part of his teaching, pause to ask yourself: "What brings me a great deal of satisfaction, pleasure, joy and happiness in life?" Once identified, then do more of that, because these activities or attitudes bring you more benefit and happiness.

It is really just that simple!

DAY 2

Giving Mindfully

The true spirit of giving is to benefit others at the expense of oneself.
—Yin Shun

Generosity and giving are important virtues in Buddhism. However, there's a right way and a less skillful way to give. Yin Shun (1905-2005), a Chinese Master, addressed ways to give mindfully offering these **Seven Don'ts When Giving**:

1. Don't give under pressure. "One may not want to give automatically but because someone comes to the door to beg (or sell), one may feel awkward about refusing and give reluctantly," Yin Shun writes. It was the "reluctant" giving which made it a weak action.
2. Don't give from fear. Avoid making a donation out of fear that you will be viewed negatively if you do not contribute.
3. Don't give from indebtedness. "Because one has obtained benefits from others, one may offer to return such kindnesses. This is merely paying a debt," Yin Shun notes.

4. Don't give expecting a reward. This applies to giving in order to be liked or to have the favor returned.
5. Don't give merely to follow family traditions. Just because your family has supported a specific charity doesn't mean you have to do the same. Doing so runs the risk of simply giving as a thoughtless, routine family habit and may lack sincerity.
6. Don't give as a way to ask for divine good fortune. This one refers to those who give to television evangelists or other spiritual leaders anticipating that their donation will later bring them a larger "blessing" or return.
7. Don't give for the sake of fame. This way of self-serving giving is evident, for example, in those who make substantial donations in order to have a building named after themselves.

Yin Shun concludes this teaching saying: "One should give properly, with deep compassion and respect."

DAY 3

Meditation and Mindfulness

Meditation brings wisdom; lack of meditation leaves ignorance.
—Buddha

A clear link between mindfulness and meditation is provided by Dr. David DeSteno, a professor of psychology at Boston's Northeastern University. He wanted to test whether or not meditation actually produced mindfulness (or greater awareness). Keeping in mind that the Buddha's "awakening" was the result of his meditation practice, Dr. DeSteno and a group of colleagues recruited thirty-nine people who were willing to take an eight-week course in meditation. None of them had practiced previously. The researchers then randomly assigned twenty recruits to take part in weekly meditation classes combined with home practice using guided recordings. The remaining nineteen were told that they had been placed on a waiting list for a future course.

After the eight-week period of instruction, test subjects were invited to the lab for an experiment that purported to examine their memory, attention and related cognitive abilities. Unknown to the members of the study group, what Dr. DeSteno wanted to know was whether there would be a difference in awareness and compassion between the meditating group and the non-meditators. To test this, he and his colleagues staged this situation. When a participant entered the lab waiting area, he/she found three chairs, two of which were already occupied. Naturally, that person sat in the free chair. As he/she waited, a fourth person—an actor—entered the room, audibly sighing in pain and using crutches and wearing a boot for a broken foot.

With no chairs available, that actor leaned against the wall. Again, unknown to the test subject, the other two people seated on chairs were also actors and had been instructed to ignore the person on crutches. Thus, the test subjects were, one by one, presented with a moral dilemma: should they give up their chair or remain seated, ignoring the suffering person's plight?

Dr. DeSteno says the results were "striking." Only sixteen percent of the non-meditating group gave up their seats while fifty percent of the meditators did. Meditation produced a mindfulness (or an awakened awareness) that increased the compassionate response threefold.

To deepen mindfulness in your daily life, consider adding times of mediation into the mix. Motivate yourself toward a meditation practice by reflecting on this wisdom from the Buddha: "Meditation brings wisdom; lack of meditation leaves ignorance. Know well what leads you forward and what holds you back and choose the path that leads to wisdom."

DAY 4

Why Not Become a Buddha?

Enjoy being a buddha. When you sit, allow the buddha in you to sit. When you walk, allow the buddha in you to walk. Enjoy your practice. If you don't become a buddha, who will?
—Thich Nhat Hanh

The Buddha was very direct and clear that he was not a god but just a human being. Therefore, the path to enlightenment and liberation that he discovered is accessible to any other human. Based on his own experience, he taught and modeled the reality that we can improve ourselves, living with purpose and happiness. The Buddha summarized his teachings in the **Noble Eightfold Path** to guide us:

1. Right view. Accept life the way it is rather than clinging to the way we wish it to be.
2. Right thought. Develop yourself to be a person who is positive and optimistic not negative and cynical.
3. Right speech. No gossip, no lying, no misrepresenting oneself and others. Very simple.
4. Right action. Respond rather than react to life.

5. Right livelihood. Do work that is right for you, for others, for the planet. The Buddha discouraged working in these five "businesses": business in weapons, business in human beings, business in meat, business in intoxicants and business in poisons.
6. Right effort. Rise daily with joy and enthusiasm. Don't give in to inertia and laziness.
7. Right mindfulness. Be present. The past is gone and the future is uncertain. Focus on now.
8. Right concentration. Meditate regularly. This practice provides a foundation of stability, peace, confidence and awareness.

DAY 5

Silence Deepens Mindfulness

*When you become aware of silence, immediately
there is that state of inner still alertness. You are present.
You have stepped out of thousands of years of
collective human conditioning.*
—Eckhart Tolle

Most people do not recognize the name Alfred Julius Emmanuel Sorensen (1890-1984). That was his birth name. Later, he would be known as Sunyata, the Buddhist word for void or emptiness.

Sorensen was the youngest child born into a Danish farming family. Operating a farm, he was expected to join the family in that endeavor, thus ending his education at eighth grade. However, the family had to sell off the farm, so Sorensen entered a four-year apprenticeship in horticulture. Working large estates in Italy, France and finally England, in 1911. Rabindranath Tagore, the famous Indian poet and mystic, visited the estate Sorensen was working on and was impressed with the quality of Sorensen's silence.

Now, think about this for a moment: what kind of quality can there be in silence that is attractive enough to be noticed and observed by others?

Tagore was so impressed with this quality that he invited Sorensen to "teach silence" at his school in India. At the age of forty, Sorensen journeyed to India and began to teach. He would remain there for more than four decades during which time he was given the name Sunyata. In India, he was a popular teacher of silence and received many visitors. However, he had no interest in popularity, power, fame or money, preferring to be alone. He built himself a stone hut in the foothills of the Himalayas (near Almora) where he lived simply.

In 1973, an American group invited him to visit and teach in California. At the age of eighty-four, he left India for California. This would become his final home where he taught "silence" until his death in 1984 at age ninety-three, the result of being struck by a car.

Silence is an important aspect for the deeper development of mindfulness, because silence brings clarity while activity often brings confusion. Consider increasing the quality of silence in your life.

Here are some ways to cultivate this silence:

- Turn off the electronics in your home one evening a week. This means no cell phone, no television, no music, no computer.
- Drive in silence. Again, no radio, no conversation.
- Eat in silence. This is a common practice in religious monasteries. Simply eat in silence, savoring your food.

- Meditate in your home. Do this several times a week beginning with as little as five minutes. Gradually increase the meditation time to fifteen or twenty minutes per session.
- Tune out distractions during the day. Do you really need to engage in small talk with colleagues or strangers? Is it necessary to fill time with speaking when you are with your partner or a friend? Can you and those close to you become comfortable with more moments of silence together?
- Rather than merely taking a vacation, consider a retreat for the same period of time. Silent retreats are offered all over the U.S. and in many foreign countries. Some retreats can be done on a long weekend; others extend for a full week and longer.

DAY 6

Managing Life According to the Buddha

Taking refuge in the Buddha, we learn to transform anger into compassion; taking refuge in the Dharma, we learn to transform delusion into wisdom; taking refuge in the Sangha, we learn to transform desire into generosity.
—Red Pine

While guiding a group meditation session, the leader asked the dozen or so present to write and complete this sentence: *Life is . . .*

Here are some of their responses: Life is difficult. Life is tough. Life is hard. Life is unpredictable. Life is disappointing. Life is frustrating. Life is complicated.

Only one person made a positive expression, writing, "Life is beautiful."

Of course, it's perfectly understandable why the majority had a negative perspective on life. Our children may cause disappointment; a spouse may leave us; our boss may not always be fair or professional; our work colleagues may be difficult.

The Buddha understood that life is indeed not always what we expect or wish it to be. For that reason, he offered three ways in which we can live a fulfilling or meaningful life in spite of the fact that it comes with strains and pains. His three-fold method is often described as "taking refuge"—finding a safe place during a time of storm. Buddhists officially describe this process as taking refuge in the "**Three Jewels**":

- the First Jewel is to take refuge in the Buddha as the guide
- the Second Jewel is to take refuge in the *dharma* (Buddhist teachings) as the path
- the Third Jewel is to take refuge in the *sangha* (Buddhist community) as companions on the path.

When we engage these three intentionally and faithfully, we find a way of putting life's changes and challenges into perspective. Those ups and downs no longer have the same power to generate great fear and anxiety. The Buddha discovered and then taught a way to overcome the fears that, left unchallenged, eat away at our peace of mind.

DAY 7

Restoring the Mind When Life is Challenging

It's a recession when your neighbor loses his job; it's a depression when you lose your own.
—Harry S. Truman

Becoming unemployed, or any other challenging setback in life, almost immediately erodes mindfulness. That's understandable. Unemployment and the task of job hunting, together with difficulties in relationships, a potential divorce, a sudden or dwindling loss of money, a serious illness, to name a few conditions, create worries . . . about paying the rent or the mortgage next month, about how quickly you can find a job, about whether or not you will find one with a comparable salary, etc.

Thus, it is vital to maintain focus and be highly mindful when job hunting. Here are five ways (five B's) to bring mindfulness to bear when unemployed or otherwise challenged.

1. **B**end. Cultivate flexibility. "Notice that the stiffest tree is the most easily cracked while the bamboo or willow survives by bending with the wind," observed Bruce Lee. Don't be rigid

about what you can do and not do. Now that you're out of work be flexible about new horizons and opportunities. Listen to everyone who has an idea or suggestion.

2. **B**ask. A dictionary definition of bask is "to revel in and make the most of something." Enjoy the journey. Don't allow yourself to see only the negative. Unemployment is an ideal opportunity to regroup, refocus and rethink. Much good can come from this period of time.

3. **B**reathe. When discouragement infects you, pause and take some intentional deep breaths as you inhale and exhale. As you breathe that way, repeat this affirmation: *I am capable. I am confident.*

4. **B**elieve in yourself. There is no doubt that being unemployed plays havoc with one's self-esteem and self-confidence. However, sooner or later most people have this unwelcome issue in their lives. And, most of them weather it, land on their feet, with many saying "it was the best thing that ever happened to me!"

5. **B**eware of your mind. The mind has a mind of its own. When unemployed it can speak to you saying you're not good enough, smart enough, experienced enough, educated enough to get a great new job. That mentality can destroy all motivation when researching, applying and

interviewing. Be aware when the mind is playing mind games with you. Stop it. Don't give in to it.

DAY 8

A Monk Named "One Drop"

*Water has become a highly precious resource.
There are some places where a barrel of water
costs more than a barrel of oil.*
—Lloyd Axworthy

Many centuries ago, a young monk was tutored by a highly regarded senior monk. In exchange for his lessons, the young monk provided services to his teacher. One of his tasks was to haul water from a nearby river, place it into a pot, heat it and then transfer the warm water into the master's tub so he could bathe.

One day, when the young monk was transferring water from the pot to the tub, he spilled several drops. The senior monk saw this and scolded him severely, telling him he was being terribly careless and completely mindless. Along with the scolding, he told the monk that even a single drop of water given to a plant could further nurture its growth. Furthermore, several drops of water could fill a jug and quench thirst, or when dropped into a pot could become a meal of soup when vegetables were added.

To his credit, the young monk got the message about water and mindfulness. He understood so completely that he took the monastic name Tekisui, meaning "One

Drop." Like his teacher, he went on to become a great Zen master.

Let's be like One Drop and take a more mindful approach to our relationship with water. Most people never pay attention to water *until* there's a problem and it's turned off. Recently, I saw this when a major water pipe broke in a nearby town. For several days, residents had no water. All restaurants had to close because they had no water. Businesses also closed because toilets could not function without water.

The fact is, most of us take water for granted. Our approach to it is often mindless. We can encourage mindfulness around water in two ways. First, by appreciating water every time we use it—showering, cooking, laundering, making tea and so on. Secondly, by conserving this valuable resource *which is not unlimited*. In many places around the planet, water is becoming scarcer and scarcer. Do your part to conserve and appreciate.

DAY 9

Being Fully Present at Work

If a man is called to be a street sweeper, he should sweep streets even as Michelangelo painted, or Beethoven composed music, or Shakespeare wrote poetry. He should sweep streets so well that all the hosts of heaven and earth will pause to say, here lived a great street sweeper who did his job well.
—Martin Luther King, Jr.

One of the greatest personalities from the twelfth century was the Jewish philosopher and scientist Maimonides (1135-1204). He was also a physician who tended carefully to all who came to him. In order to do his work mindfully, it is said that he authored and then offered this prayer upon rising each day:

> Before I begin the Holy Work of healing the creation of your hands, I place my eternity before the throne of Your glory, that you grant me strength of spirit and fortitude to faithfully execute my work.
>
> Let not desire for wealth or benefit blind me from seeing truth. Deem me worthy of seeing in the sufferer who seeks my advice a person—neither rich nor poor, friend or foe, good man or bad; show me only the person.

If doctors wiser than I seek to help me understand, grant me the desire to learn from them, for the knowledge of healing is boundless. But when fools deride me, give me fortitude. Let my love for my profession strengthen my resolve to withstand the derision even of people of high station.

Illuminate the way for me, for any lapse in my knowledge can bring illness and death upon your creations. I ask You, merciful and gracious God, strengthen me in body and soul, and instill within me a perfect spirit.

How much more meaningful would our work be if we approached it with the same spirit of humility and mindfulness as did Maimonides. In our work—whatever it may be—can we train ourselves to see "only the person?" Can we be willing to learn from others in our place of work; from those above us as well as those below us? Can we allow our commitment to be faithful workers withstand criticism from others?

DAY 10

For More Inner Peace Clean Your House

A monk's day begins with cleaning. We sweep the Temple grounds and gardens, we polish the main Temple Hall. We don't do it because it's dirty or messy. We do it to eliminate gloom in our hearts.
—Shoukei Matsumoto

Many mental health counselors advise their patients to clean their living areas. That's because a sloppy, chaotic home reflects an inner chaos and unhappiness. Shoukei Matsumoto, a Buddhist monk and author of *A Monk's Guide to a Clean House and Mind*, explains that cleaning and maintaining a neat, tidy environment are a vital aspect of Buddhist practice in Japan. "In Japanese Buddhism, it is said that what you must do in the pursuit of your spirituality is clean, clean, clean. This is because the practice of cleaning is powerful," he notes.

Here's what this Buddhist monk learned about the spiritual practice of cleaning:

- Cleaning practice—that is sweeping, polishing, wiping, tidying, washing—constitutes an important step toward inner peace.

- Buddhism does not separate the person from the environment and cleaning expresses both respect and unity with the world around us.
- Cleaning when done mindfully is a powerful meditation practice. For that reason, Japanese Buddhist monks routinely clean their own temples. Cleaning is not just a job but another meditation technique, not one to be "outsourced" to a custodial service.
- There is no end to cleaning just as there is no ending of or "graduation" in meditation practice. Shortly after we vacuum and sweep floors and carpets, they become soiled again. Dust accumulates. In the same way, after we end a meditation round and feel peaceful and calm, it's not long before some irritation emerges or anxiety is aroused.

Shoukei Matsumoto suggests that, after cleaning up your home, apartment or room, you extend the spiritual practice of cleaning into other life areas. His recommendation is stimulating. What if we began to tidy up our relationships and friendships to make them "cleaner"? Or, how about cleaning up the way we drive our vehicles, making roadways and traffic less anxiety-producing? Or, how about cleaning up the way we treat people who serve us—baristas, store clerks, bank tellers, waiters and waitresses, flight attendants, and so on. Doing this kind of cleaning, you can help eliminate the gloom in the world.

DAY 11

Embracing Child-Like Curiosity

Never lose a holy curiosity.
—Albert Einstein

In 1941, on a beautiful summer day in Switzerland, a man was walking with his dog along some mountain trails. Both returned home to find burrs stuck to the dog's fur and to the man's clothing. This oddity fascinated the man who carefully picked out a few burrs placing them under a microscope. There he could clearly see that the burs were covered in tiny hooks that clung onto the loops in his trousers and onto his dog's fur.

From that day's outing, the man, an electrical engineer named George de Mestral, developed the idea of creating a product made up of two sheets of material. One sheet would have hooks while the other would have the loops. Today, this product, Velcro, is regarded as a great scientific creation of modern times. Velcro is commonly used across a wide range of industries and services, including clothing, footwear, military, hospitals, space exploration, automotive and recreation.

It was De Mestral's mindfulness about burrs that led to this amazingly useful invention. Curiosity is one common denominator to all great inventors. And curiosity is an important aspect of mindfulness for these reasons:

- Curiosity makes your mind active not passive
- Curiosity keeps your mind observant and attentive
- Curiosity opens you up to fresh insights and new possibilities
- Curiosity prevents you from being on automatic pilot
- Curiosity helps you see the big picture
- Curiosity forces you to ask "Why?"

Children, like inventors, are deeply curious. Unfortunately, this child-like characteristic is lost to most adults.

Strengthen your mindfulness by reclaiming your curiosity.

DAY 12

Attend Your Own Funeral

> *When one is actually dying it is a bit late to begin thinking seriously about death. We should familiarize ourselves with the thought long before we hope it will happen!*
> —Maurice Walshe

Though it sounds dark and unpleasant, the Buddhist tradition has strongly stressed the importance of thinking about one's own death. The reason: a meditation on death is a powerful tool for developing insight into the best way of living a meaningful, significant and satisfying life. The Dalai Lama says: "The illusion of permanence, or being unaware of death, creates the counter-productive idea that you will be around for a long time: this, in turn, leads to superficial activities that undermine both yourself and others."

One way to begin this type of meditation is to imagine yourself in attendance at your own funeral. If you can overcome any reluctance about this exercise to attend your own funeral, then consider:

- Who do you think would come by to offer condolences?
- Who would surprise you by being there?

- Who would disappoint you by not being there?
- Who would conduct your funeral service and why that person?
- Which individuals would be invited to share a few words about you?
- What positive things might those speakers say about you?
- Look back upon your own life …
    - did you focus too much on wealth, prestige, success?
    - did you worry too much?
    - did you tell the people you loved that you loved them?
    - did you work at something you found meaningless?
    - from this perspective, what would you do differently?

Here's one final question to ask yourself frequently from time to time: If this was the last day of my life … what would I do? what would I say? who would I be with?

DAY 13

Be a Guru to Someone

What would this world be like if there were no Guru or guides?
—Swami Jyotirmayanada

The word "guru" comes from two Sanskrit words: *guha* which means cave and *ru* which means light. Combined, guru simply means someone who brings light to the cave. This is, in fact, one standard definition of a guru as "transmitter of light."

Here's a meditation to do on the word "guru": First, sit quietly and identify those who have brought light to your cave. Pause and silently express gratitude to those individuals living or deceased. Secondly, continue to sit quietly and identify people you know whose cave needs light. Offer this Buddhist lovingkindness meditation:

May (name) be happy.
May (name) be healthy.
May (name) be safe.
May (name) be free of suffering.

End your meditation by considering how you could be the person who can bring light to their cave. What form would that light take: A text or email of encouragement? An invitation to join you for tea, coffee and conversation? An opportunity to walk and talk together? A kind expression of your ongoing love and support?

DAY 14

Responding Versus Reacting

Examine thus yourself from every side.
Note harmful thoughts and every futile striving.
Thus it is that heroes in the bodhisattva path
Apply the remedies to keep a steady mind.
—Shantideva

At an inner-city school in California, a five-week experimental program in mindfulness was conducted with fifth-grade students. A mindfulness coach came twice a week and led fifteen-minute meditation sessions with a focus on breath and concentration on a single object.

The goal was simple: rather than merely telling children to pay attention, mindfulness meditation would teach them *how* to do that. Then the students were asked to apply mindfulness on the school playground where they were to cultivate compassion and reflect on their emotions before lashing out at someone.

After only a few mindfulness sessions, one boy told his classmates: "I was losing at baseball and I was about to throw a bat, but the mindfulness really helped." Another student, when asked to explain mindfulness, said it's "not hitting someone in the mouth."

Though mindfulness can be explained and defined in many ways, these fifth graders offer one way to understand the concept, namely, that *mindfulness is the ability to make better decisions.* The reason is simple. When we are mindful, we create a space between a reaction and a response. And in that space we can access the wisdom that empowers us to move from reaction to reflection to response. Unlike a reaction, in which we are controlled by difficult thoughts and emotions, mindfulness creates a gap moment that allows us to control the response. In the gap we can pause, analyze and respond in a way that is skillful, positive and helpful. It's what Shantideva calls keeping a "steady mind." This is good to remember whenever we begin to feel frustration and anger rising.

DAY 15

Live Like a Zen Monk

When walking, walk. When eating, eat.
—Zen Proverb

This may be the most user-friendly definition of mindfulness: when walking, walk; when eating, eat. This proverb offers a simplicity for living combined with a mindfulness for every daily activity.

Too often, when we walk we're not paying attention to the walking. As we walk, we are preoccupied with other mental activities, usually a negative one—anxiety, anger, fear, hurt, disappointment, etc. A Zen master would advise, "Let all that go and just enjoy the walk by focusing on the walk."

Likewise, when we eat we're not paying attention to the eating. We often consume an entire meal completely unaware of what we've eaten, how much we've eaten and how quickly we have eaten. Again, a Zen master would say, "Pay attention to your food. Smell it; savor it; enjoy it mouthful by mouthful."

This Zen proverb of six words is mindfulness in a nutshell: *When walking, walk. When eating, eat.* It reminds us to do one thing at a time; to do it slowly; to do it deliberately; and to do it completely. This can and ought to be expanded into daily life. Here are some ways:

- When listening to a friend, listen.
- When mowing your lawn, mow.
- When loading the dishwasher, load.
- When sitting with your cat, sit.
- When driving, drive.
- When working, work.

By approaching daily living this way, you'll discover the joy of living like a Zen monk because your daily mindfulness will bring you calm, peace, perspective and tranquility.

DAY 16

Blessings in Disguise

I would merely beg you not to be too much bowed down by grief. What seem to us bitter trials are often blessings in disguise.
—Oscar Wilde

A man was asked to put together a list of things he was grateful for. Though he was a person with many admirable achievements and accomplishments, his gratitude list was as remarkable as it was unusual. His list included the following:

1. his first job upon graduating from college as a high school janitor
2. being laid off from a job due to a bad economy
3. a diagnosis of melanoma
4. all the people who did not believe in him.

He explained that each one of those "burdens" were actually blessings in disguise. Here's why:

1. Working as a janitor led him to his future wife, the daughter of a fellow janitor.
2. Being laid off forced him to jumpstart his career as a book illustrator.

3. His cancer diagnosis prompted him to organize events promoting melanoma awareness.
4. All those people who were negative, cynical and critical further fueled his determination to succeed.

The lesson in that man's approach is a powerful one: we must not be hasty in judging as unwelcome situations come crashing into our lives. Rather, we ought to remain open and curious with the conviction that "bitter trials are often blessings in disguise."

DAY 17

Doing Your Very Best

*Don't waste your time striving for perfection;
instead, strive for excellence—doing your best.*
—Lawrence Olivier

A young man from Sydney, Australia tells of receiving the best advice of his life. During a time when he felt lost in life, he heard about a prominent meditation teacher at a Buddhist monastery in Thailand. So, he decided to visit the monk and ask him some questions. It took the young man eight hours to get to Bangkok from Sydney and then a ten-hour train trip, followed by a taxi ride to the monk's monastery.

Tired but excited, he entered the monastery and learned that the monk he sought was actually the abbot, who, at that very moment, was giving a public lecture. Making his way to where the abbot was teaching, he joined a large audience of monks and army officers, poor farmers and wealthy merchants, village women in rags and well-dressed women from Bangkok.

The Australian sat down among the crowd waiting for his opportunity to address the monk, but, after several hours and feeling discouraged, he got up and left. Walking through the monastery grounds toward the main gate, the man saw some monks sweeping the grounds. Because he had another hour before his taxi returned, he decided to pick up a broom and help them sweep. About twenty minutes later, while he was busy sweeping, he felt a hand on his shoulder. Turning around, he was shocked to see that the hand belonged to the abbot, who had noticed him in the crowd and was aware he didn't have an opportunity to ask questions. Because the abbot was on his way to another appointment, he paused in front of the young Australian and said something quickly in Thai, then left. The abbot's assistant interpreted for the young man: "Our abbot says that if you are going to sweep, give it everything you've got."

The man returned to Australia and became quite successful and happy with his life because he took that advice making it his life mantra: "Whatever you are doing, give it everything you've got."

That insight is applicable for us in all of life's situations. For example:

- If you're married or in a relationship, give it everything you've got.
- If you're an executive, give it everything you've got.
- If you're dealing with cancer and being treated for it, give it everything you've got.
- If you're a social worker or therapist, give it everything you've got.

- If you're a photographer, a poet, an artist, a musician, etc., give it everything you've got.

DAY 18

Living the Four Noble Truths

*The Four Noble Truths are pragmatic rather than dogmatic.
They suggest a course of action to be followed rather than
a set of dogmas to be believed.*
—Stephen Batchelor

One of the first lessons the Buddha taught after his enlightenment or insight was about suffering. This teaching contained what came to be known as the "four noble truths." Traditionally, they are stated this way:

- The truth of suffering
- The truth of the origin of suffering
- The truth of the cessation of suffering
- The truth of the path to the cessation of suffering

These can be phrased in more modern terminology:

- There is suffering.
- The cause of suffering can be identified.
- Once identified, suffering can be treated.
- Suffering can be ended.

The Four Noble Truths have an amazing relevance and applicability to daily life when considered mindfully. Here's an example: A man is diagnosed with lung cancer—the first noble truth. His cancer was likely brought on by a life-long habit of smoking—the second noble truth. A doctor tells him that, fortunately, his cancer can be treated—the third noble truth. Finally, his route to healing or an end to his suffering can be accomplished if he receives medical treatment, quits smoking, exercises regularly and eats healthy foods.

Here is another example. A woman is an alcoholic, which has negatively impacted her family, friends, job and social circle—the first noble truth. Though she never intended to become an alcoholic, it began when she was experiencing emotional pain and turned to alcohol as a relief—the second noble truth. Following the advice of friends, she begins to participate regularly in an addiction recovery group—the third noble truth. Within a few months she is no longer drinking, is restoring many of her damaged relationships and is increasingly at peace with herself—the fourth noble truth.

In both cases, it is important to note that it's not only action which is essential for removing suffering but carefully examining the mind which allowed suffering to emerge in the first place. Today is the perfect day to look at your own life and lifestyle. If there is a part of you which is not in harmony, work with the four noble truths to create greater symmetry and tranquility.

DAY 19

Let Questions Open Your Mind

In life it is more important to ask the right questions than to have the right answers.
—Victor M. Parachin

A man tells of attending a silent ten-day retreat. On opening day, the meditation leader met privately with him and asked: "How is the world treating you?" The man responded with a polite, trite comment that things were going OK. Then the meditation teacher asked him this follow-up question: "And how are you treating the world?"

It was this second question that impacted the man and made him realize, "I had a lot to learn about what I was *really* doing with my life."

Put yourself in his place. Assume an insightful person asks you, "How is the world treating you?" Carefully answer the question.

Then, listen to the next question: "How are you treating the world?" Again, think it through and answer the question.

As you work on those two questions, be mindful that questions such as these, wisely asked by a meditation instructor, are useful tools for giving birth to new insights. Pay special attention to which of the two questions elicits a deeper response and evokes greater insight.

DAY 20

Move From Fear to Curiosity

Fear is sand in the machinery of life.
—E. Stanley Jones

In 1911, a man called Ishi, the last member of the Yahi Native American tribe, emerged from the hills near Oroville, California. He had spent his life hiding in fear of whites because they had systematically slaughtered his tribe. After forty years of hiding, he came forth hungry and lonely. Fortunately, the local sheriff took him into custody for his own protection. Called a "wild man" in news reports, Ishi became the object of interest to thousands of onlookers including anthropology professors at the University of California, Berkeley. They provided him with permanent housing and interviewed him at length to learn more about Native American customs.

When Ishi was taken on a visit to San Francisco, it meant boarding a train in Oroville. As the train pulled into the station, Ishi observed for a moment and then hid behind a pillar. When it was time to board the train, his hosts called him over and together they all stepped aboard.

Later, Ishi told his companions that trains frightened him and his entire tribe, explaining that whenever they saw a train, they thought it was a demon that ate people because of the way it snaked along, bellowing smoke and fire. His hosts were both shocked and surprised that he would actually get onto the train, so they asked: "How did you have courage to just step onto the train if your believed it was a dangerous demon?" His answer is highly instructive: "My life has taught me to be more curious than afraid."

Apply Ishi's response to daily living in these ways:

- Rather than fear the future, remain open and curious.
- Rather than fear a serious life challenge, remain open and curious.
- Rather than fear a journey through grief and loss, remain open and curious.
- Rather than fear life, remain open and curious about the ways it unfolds for you.

DAY 21

Expanding Your Circle of Kindness

Kindness is a habit that anyone can cultivate.
—Victor M. Parachin

Tragically, an elderly man had a fall that resulted in paralysis. Fortunately, he had a good friend who spent time caring for the man—feeding him, cleaning him, rolling him over. Others commented on how kind this caregiver was to his friend. After hearing similar comments several times, the good friend made this observation: "When a baby needs round-the-clock care, we find it natural and no one comments on it. However, when an old man needs the same round-the-clock care, people find it unfortunate, tragic and even distasteful." Then, he added this piercing comment: "Why don't we simply recognize that a person needs help and ask how we can be of service?"

The paralyzed man's friend is an example of someone who has expanded his capacity for kindness. His is an example more should follow. Too many times, kindness is extended only toward the familiar and the convenient: family, friends, or people of the same race, nationality, gender. While this kindness is good, consider expanding it to those less familiar and less convenient.

Simply recognize when a person needs help and extend yourself no matter who they are, no matter what their level of wealth or poverty, no matter their behavior and beliefs.

Authentic kindness is extended to all beings. And, kindness is a habit anyone can cultivate. It just takes practice. Begin today!

DAY 22

The Joy Of Generosity

If you knew, as I do, the power of giving, you would not let a single meal pass without sharing some of it.
—Buddha

A dictionary definition of generosity reads this way: the quality of being kind, understanding, and not selfish: the quality of being generous; *especially*: willingness to give money and other valuable things to others.

Buddhist tradition notes that the Buddha himself taught three fundamental types of generosity. First, material generosity, which involves sharing money and other material things with others. Secondly, emotional generosity, which the Buddha described as "making others feel unafraid." We do this when we spend time with a person who has just experienced a traumatic event such as the diagnosis of a life-threatening illness, or with someone who has had a loss to death, or with someone who has been "downsized." Thirdly, there is the generosity of sharing wisdom with others such as leading a meditation group, offering a spiritual workshop, making a presentation about higher values and ethics.

The Buddha often taught about the importance of generosity because it is not only helpful to the recipient of our generosity. We ourselves are greatly helped when we act generously. Generosity is a powerful virtue because it enables us to counteract three Buddhist poisons: ignorance, attachment and aversion. When we are generous, we free ourselves from that poison of grasping attachment and let go. Gandhi wisely said: "The fragrance remains in the hand that gives the rose."

Bottom line: via generosity we free others from suffering *and* we free ourselves from suffering.

DAY 23

Become Your Inner Choir Director

Make it a daily habit to explore, examine and evaluate your self-talk.
—Victor M. Parachin

There are many voices inside our minds, all of them crying out for attention. Get to know your unique inner talk so that you can effectively control it, much like the way a choir director leads a group of singers. What kind of voices are in your head? Are they sad, negative, joyless, frustrated, dispirited ones? Are they happy, positive, joyful, peaceful, passionate ones? Most of us have a blend of the two extremes.

Those two extremities are often impacted by external circumstances. When we succeed at something, there is an inevitable uplift. The positive voices emerge. When we experience suffering, there is an inevitable disappointment. Then, the negative voices emerge. With practice, we begin to build awareness of mind, leading to awareness of emotions. All of us can make emotionally-intelligent thinking our default mode.

Take charge of your inner dialogue. When disturbing and negative voices emerge, notice them without judging them harshly, and direct them gently to soften and ease up. Simultaneously, pay attention to the voices that express gratitude, joy, compassion, kindness, love, peace, strength, humor. Allow them to "sing out" more clearly and loudly. Direct your voices toward hope, happiness, harmony and your life will reflect those very qualities.

DAY 24

Fitting In is Overrated!

*One's own duty, performed imperfectly,
is better than doing another's duty perfectly.*
—Bhagavad Gita (3.35)

If you're like most people, the chances are good that you've spent far too much time trying to fit it. It's a huge waste of time which brings nothing but irritation, frustration and disappointment, because ultimately, we can never really fit in, no matter how hard we try.

Why?

Because it's impossible to be everything we think everyone else wants, needs and demands that we be. Trying and trying and trying to fit in and be acceptable to others leaves us feeling compromised, emotionally and intellectually weak and completely lacking in authenticity. Our true voice may not get lost but may become a quiet whisper.

How about doing this instead: stop trying to fit in. While continuing to be intentional about extending kindness, civility, compassion to all those you meet and relate to, decline the pressure to fit in. Allow yourself to follow paths that speak to your spirit, regardless of the culture around. This simple decision will serve you well.

Give it a try. Here are some words of wisdom to guide you:

- "As the saying goes, you might as well be yourself; everyone else is taken."—Robert Bly
- "If you're always trying to be normal, you'll never know how amazing you are."—Maya Angelou
- "We're so quick to cut away pieces of ourselves to suit a particular relationship, a job, a circle of friends, incessantly editing who we are until we fit in."—Charles de Lint

DAY 25

Thought Transplants

*When presented with disquieting thoughts
or feelings, cultivate an opposite elevated attitude.*
—Patanjali

Think about "disquieting" thoughts. A quick list could include anger, anxiety, jealousy, rage, distrust, powerlessness, hopelessness, sadness, disappointment and more. In fact, psychologists claim that we humans have a wide range of emotions. Some listing of emotions contains 1000 different human feelings.

Patanajali, an ancient sage, was aware of this unique human ability to feel so many things in so many ways. Thus, he offers the concept of "thought transplant" suggesting that we don't have to remain with negative, self-sabotaging thoughts. Rather, those hurting and haunting thoughts can simply be replaced with "an opposite elevated attitude."

When he uses the phrase "elevated attitude" he is promoting the power of positive thinking. Here's how to cultivate this way of thinking:

- Rather than view yourself as weak, view yourself as strong.

- Rather than view yourself as timid, view yourself as confident.
- Rather than view yourself as frightened, view yourself as courageous.
- Rather than view yourself as unlovable, view yourself as loveable.
- Rather than view yourself as unable, view yourself as able.
- Rather than view yourself as . . . (You fill in the blanks)

That's how to engage in thought transplants.

DAY 26

Dealing With Mind Forgeries

*Beware you do not lose the substance
by grasping at the shadow.*
—Aesop

Have you ever considered the differences between helping and serving?

- niceness and kindness?
- seriousness and sincerity?
- tolerance and inclusiveness?

Some people go through life believing they are serving when they're merely helping. Why? Because serving arises out of humility while helping can emerge from superiority.

Some people go through life believing they are kind when they are merely nice. Why? Because niceness often emerges out of a need to be liked. Niceness is forced forward by the mind. Kindness arises spontaneously and without motive. It is an unforced activity.

Some people go through life with great seriousness but lack sincerity. How does this happen? Because seriousness is attached to secondary intentions. It comes from the mind. Sincerity is unattached to other motives and comes from the heart.

Some people go through life practicing tolerance but never inclusiveness. Why does this happen? Because tolerance contains judgment. If someone says to us: "I am tolerating you," we would not feel that as a warm, affirming position. However, when we hear the phrase "you're included!" we recognize that as welcoming.

Becoming mindful of these mind forgeries will encourage you in the transition from helping to serving, from niceness to kindness, from seriousness to sincerity and from tolerance to inclusiveness.

DAY 27

Deepening Your Spiritual Side

*The Bhagavad-Gita has a profound influence on
the spirit of mankind by its devotion to God
which is manifested by actions.*
—Albert Schweitzer

The Bhagavad Gita, or just "Gita" as it is often referred to, is an essential Hindu sacred text. Believed to have been composed in the first century CE, it has inspired such diverse people as Mahatma Gandhi, T. S. Eliot, Ralph Waldo Emerson, Albert Schweitzer and Henry David Thoreau. In it, the God Krishna leads the warrior Arjuna to a higher and deeper understanding of his spiritual nature and how that is to work itself out in daily life.

For those who believe in a Higher Power, the Gita offers these four "yogic" ways of deepening a connection to the Divine.

1. Through the *intellect*. If your style is to research, read, study than your best access to the Divine is via those intellectual approaches. This one is called *Jnana yoga*.
2. Through the *heart*. If your style is a heartfelt approach to life, then your best access to the

Divine is through adoration and expressions of love for the Divine. This one is called *Bhakti yoga*.
3. Through *action*. If your style is one of energetic activity, then your best access to the Divine is via serving others and offering that as your commitment to the Divine. This one is called *Karma yoga*.
4. Through the *mind*. If you are a reflective and introspective person, then your best access to the Divine is through meditation. This one is called *Raja yoga*.

The Gita recognizes that every person has his or her own unique spiritual style. When seeking to deepen your connection to Divinity, tap into your strength and lead with your strong suit.

DAY 28

You Are In Charge Of Your Life

*The mind can train itself to abandon unskillful qualities—
defilements such as greed, aversion, delusion, and
harmfulness—and to develop skillful qualities,
free of these defilements, in their place.*
—Thanissaro Bhikkhu

In some religious traditions, the fallen nature of the human is emphasized, along with the need for salvation. The Buddha and the religion that bears his name, however, sees only suffering and a way to end suffering.

There's a huge difference between the two views.

Buddhism teaches that we humans have "Buddha nature" and all we need to do is recognize, respond and realize our true nature. The Buddha's perspective is more "people friendly," reminding us that we are in charge of our lives and the direction in which we wish to move. In fact, the Buddha taught that the way to tap into our Buddha nature and end suffering is to engage in these three actions. (Dhammapada, 183 / Chapter 14)

First, to cease from negative actions. This involves "abstaining" from taking life, from taking what is not freely given, from engaging in sexual misconduct, from using false speech, from taking intoxicants which cloud the mind.

Secondly, to do what is good. This involves cultivating practices such as generosity, ethics, patience, gratitude, compassion and wisdom.

Thirdly, to purify and strengthen the mind. This means developing and deepening meditation because that is where we learn to use the mind skillfully.

Buddhism clearly and consistently promotes a positive view of human beings teaching that we have the power to change our lives at any time and that we are in charge of how we live.

DAY 29

Search Others For Their Virtues

Never miss an opportunity of seeing anything beautiful.
—Ralph Waldo Emerson

If you want to be happier, more content, more confident, more productive and feel far less stressed, take this one simple step: search others for their virtues. This is actually a quote from Benjamin Franklin, one of the wisest sages in early America. His advice to "search others for their virtues" is powerful and positive.

Too often, people spend time seeing others' flaws, faults and failings. As a result, many people are left deflated and debilitated, feeling they're not good enough, smart enough, successful enough, fast enough. Could it be that one reason why stress and anxiety levels are so high is because we live in an ocean of emotional negativity?

You can change that!

Search others for their virtues.

Train yourself to see the good, the positive, the noble, the heroic in others.

Everyone has virtues such as loyalty, patience, perseverance, kindness, compassion, generosity, fairness, faithfulness.

Shift your perspective from seeing weakness and shortcomings to seeing strength and substance in others. Remember to include yourself in this shifting view.

DAY 30

Using Your Mind Skillfully

Who is your enemy? Mind is your enemy.
Who is your friend? Mind is your friend.
—Buddha

This quote, attributed to the Buddha, clearly shows that how we think can either help us or hurt us. So, the next time you face a problem do this: don't add to the problem.

- Don't add fear.
- Don't add anxiety.
- Don't add confusion.
- Don't add anger.
- Don't add shame.
- Don't add frustration.
- Don't add outrage.
- Don't add indignation.
- Don't add resentment.

Just deal with the problem as it is. Use your mind constructively not destructively to help resolve the issue at hand.

DAY 31

Don't Look Around

Comparison is the thief of joy.
—Theodore Roosevelt

An American man completed Zen training in Japan and was given the gift of a monk's robe by his teacher. Inside the robe, his teacher carefully embroidered this final piece of advice: Don't look around.

The teacher was a true Zen master because that short sentence, if applied, can prevent a wide variety of misery that we bring upon ourselves when we do look around. It's a reminder to . . .

- Tend your own garden.
- Mind your own business.
- Don't compete.
- Don't compare.
- Be focused on your life.

Don't compare yourself to some external, vague standard of success and happiness. Look within. Dig deep. Everything you need for growing in wisdom will be found within not without.

DAY 32

How To Become Dis-Illusioned

Illusions are actually delusions.
—Victor M. Parachin

We live in an ocean of illusion, full of false paths, false values, false ideas. Our diverse and creative illusions take many forms:

- I'll be happy when . . . (Reality: The ideal time to be happy isn't in the future—it's now, in the present moment.)
- I'll start exercising, dieting, quit smoking, drinking . . . soon . . . (Reality: Commitments delayed are commitments denied.)
- I'll do that when I have more time . . . (Reality: If something is important to us, we make the time.)
- I'll get there faster if . . . (Reality: Speeding up and rushing diminish our chances of enjoying the journey.)
- I can change him/her . . . (Reality: The only person you can change is yourself.)
- I have control over . . . (Reality: The only control you have is over your mind.)

- I'm a self-made man/woman . . . (Reality: There's been help from others along the way.)
- She/he had instant success . . . (Reality: There's no such thing. Most often, success is based on the foundation of persistent, persevering hard work.)
- I'll make a donation when I have more money . . . (Reality: Generosity is a matter of the heart not a bank account. If the heart isn't a generous one, there will never be enough money to make a donation.)

Because illusions surround us and impact our minds, today is the perfect day to begin the process of becoming dis-illusioned.

DAY 33

When Things Go Wrong...

Your living is determined not so much by what life brings to you as by the attitude you bring to life; not so much by what happens to you as by the way your mind looks at what happens.
—Kahlil Gibran

When things go wrong... don't go wrong with them.

It's easy to say "yes" to life when everything is easy, comfortable, good. However, the challenge emerges the moment life becomes rough. When things go wrong, don't go wrong with them: maintain the right mind, the right thoughts, the right words and the right actions. For example:

- If a relationship ends, watch the tendency to wallow in anger.
- If you lose a loved one to death, avoid letting bitterness triumph.
- If there is the diagnosis of a life-threatening illness, what value is there in railing against life's injustice?
- If you are betrayed by a good friend, resist the resentment that can rule your life.
- If you are downsized, embracing cynicism will not soften the blow.

Whenever things go wrong, pause, take a deep breath, consider all possibilities and begin to move forward.

DAY 34

Make Today Count

Yesterday is gone. Tomorrow is a mystery.
Today is a gift. Live out this day with awakened joy.
—Victor M. Parachin

Each evening at the Zen Mountain Monastery in New York these words are chanted prior to a period of meditation:

> Let me respectfully remind you,
> Life and death are of supreme importance.
> Time swiftly passes by and opportunities are lost.
> Each of us should strive to awaken . . . awaken
> Take heed.
> Do not squander your life.

There is a similar expression found in the Bible, book of Psalms (118:24): This is the day the Lord has made...rejoice and be glad in it.

Both the Buddhist and the Biblical wisdom remind us that every single day is a gift. We should not waste energy in regrets about the past nor fears about the future but simply, purely, live awakened joy in the present day.

DAY 35

Top Ten Reasons to Meditate

It is helpful to remind yourself that meditation is about opening and relaxing with whatever arises, without picking and choosing.
—Pema Chödrön

10. Meditation improves physical health.
9. Meditation improves mental health.
8. Meditation improves spiritual health.
7. Meditation deepens intuition.
6. Meditation generates feelings of peace.
5. Meditation increases self-awareness.
4. Meditation increases creativity.
3. Meditation increases spontaneity.
2. Meditation makes it easier to get along with others.
1. Meditation makes you easier to get along with.

Pick a reason and begin. Also, consider finding and joining with a group for meditation. If there isn't one in your community, start one yourself.

DAY 36

Give Everyone an "A"

*Do more for the world than the world does for you.
That is success.*
—Henry Ford

Actually, don't just give everyone an "A" . . . but three! *A*cknowledge, *A*ffirm and *A*ppreciate others every day.

So many people we contact feel stressed, anxious, tense, unhappy. Be the one who generates a more positive life moment for them by:

- Making strong eye contact. This tells the person you *acknowledge* them and are not distracted by the environment. Eye contact also tells them you are friendly and engaged.
- Smiling at them. This tells them you are *affirming* them. And, when you smile, it is highly likely they will smile back, making the brief encounter friendlier and warmer. "A warm smile is the universal language of kindness," said author William Arthur Ward.
- Thanking them. This tells them you *appreciate* them, their time, their service. Alice Walker says: "Thank you expresses extreme gratitude, humility, understanding."

DAY 37

Beware About "Bragging Rights"

*There is a difference between conceit and confidence.
Conceit is bragging about yourself. Confidence means
you believe you can get the job done.*
—Johnny Unitas

There was once a turtle who lived in the woods. One day he overheard two hunters discussing how they were going to catch turtles the very next day. The turtle ran to his friends, the cranes, for help.

"Oh, beautiful birds and good friends," the turtle said, "hunters are planning to capture turtles tomorrow. I need your help to escape the forest. I am unable to fly, but if you each hold the end of a stick in your beak, then I will bite the middle, and you can lift me safely away."

"Alright," said the cranes. "But you'd better bite down extra tight so we don't lose you. You mustn't speak a word! Do not let go!"

"Don't worry," said the turtle "I won't."

The next morning the turtle bit down on a long stick and the cranes carried him together, soaring high above the trees. Then, a group of people, seeing the two cranes and the turtle high in the air, shouted out down below.

"Look at those clever birds! They managed to carry a turtle!"

The proud, talkative turtle opened his mouth saying, "This was my idea." He tumbled down to earth.

Beware of "bragging rights." Being driven by ego can be dangerous. Bragging can cause a self-inflicted wound.

DAY 38

Focus on Progress Not Perfection

*Striving for excellence motivates you;
striving for perfection is demoralizing.*
—Harriet Braiker

Perfectionism isn't good. It's unhealthy. There's an enormous difference between having high standards and being a perfectionist. That difference shows up as distress, anxiety and frustration.

Perfectionism is a kind of personality disorder that is harmful to oneself and others. For example, expect perfection from your partner and your relationship will soon be in trouble. Expect perfection from your children or your parents and you will live with deep disappointment combined with anger.

Perfectionism is a phobia, the fear of making a mistake; the fear of failure; the fear of disapproval.

Perfectionism is the false view that a mistake is a crisis, a catastrophe.

Perfectionism suggests a state of flawlessness, without any defects. As such it's totally unrealistic and unattainable.

Perfectionism has links to depression, anxiety disorders, anorexia, obsessive-compulsive disorder, insomnia.

The antidote to perfectionism is as simple as it is profound—focus on progress not perfection!

And, accept imperfection in yourself and in others.

DAY 39

Ten Rules For Kindness

Be kind whenever possible.
It's always possible.
—14th Dalai Lama

Many elementary schools post "Rules for Kindness" to guide the children. The list—usually scripted in bold letters, and placed on a wall that students walk by several times a day—often includes "kindness rules" such as:

- Be kind and gentle in all things.
- Respect others.
- Everyone gets to play.
- No violence in word or deed.
- No put downs, only pull ups.
- No exclusive behavior ("you can't play with us").
- Treat people the way you want to be treated.
- Don't hurt others on the inside or the outside.
- Help others when they need help.
- Treat *everybody* with kindness.

Adults can profit from these same rules. Try it. Each week, for the next ten weeks, take one of these rules for kindness and apply it daily. Use the "kindness rule for the week" as a guideline for your choices and for your behavior.

DAY 40

Thomas Jefferson's Meditation Practice

I have two doctors, my left leg and my right.
—G.M. Trevelyan

Thomas Jefferson, who lived to be eighty-three at a time when the average life expectancy was just around forty, walked four miles every day. He journaled that, for him, the purpose of walking was to "relax the mind."

A four-mile walk takes around sixty to seventy minutes. It not only refreshes and strengthens the body but does the same for the mind when walking is used as meditation. There are many approaches to transforming walking into walking-meditation. Here are two of my favorites:

1. Just walk and observe. Be truly mindful, noticing the path, the grasses, the trees and shrubs, insects, birds. On such a meditation walk one day, I encountered one of the largest turtles I'd seen making his way to a water refuge. On the way back, I came across a mother raccoon gently guiding her three young ones across the path into a forested area.

2. When walking you can give your mind a focus by a simple method of counting with your steps. As you walk, count the times your right foot touches the ground beginning with three steps: 1, 2, 3. Once at 3, add another number and begin again: 1, 2, 3, 4. Once at 4, add another number and begin again: 1, 2, 3, 4, 5. Follow this pattern until you get to number 10. Then, do the same with the left leg and keep alternating the legs. Once you feel your mind is relaxed, stop counting. If you find yourself overly preoccupied with thoughts start up the count again.

DAY 41

Peaceful Heart and a Happy Mind

It's never too late to have a happy childhood.
—Berke Breathed

The Buddhist teacher Pema Chödrön tells of a time when her children were teenagers and she took them to meet a high-ranking Tibetan Lama. Because her children were not Buddhists and knew very little about Buddhism, she asked the Lama to offer them some wisdom that didn't require them to have any understanding of the Buddhist path. Without hesitating, he told them: "You are going to die; and when you do, you will take nothing with you but your state of mind."

While no one knows for certain exactly what happens at the time of death, the Lama's comment is worth thinking about and acting upon. If, in fact, it's true that all we take along at the time of death is our state of mind, why not begin now to cultivate a peaceful heart and a happy mind? If, in fact, it's true that all we take along at the time of death is our state of mind, why not take a peaceful, happy spirit rather than a frustrated and angry one?

Cultivating a peaceful heart and a happy mind is not difficult and involves these ingredients:

- Living spaciously, that is, keeping your surroundings as well as your daily schedule open enough to allow for breathing space. Use that open space for meditation, contemplation and spiritual growth.
- Managing anger. There's a lot of be angry about and there are many people who will anger us.
- Practicing non-harming and non-violence toward *all* beings: people, animals, insects, fish, birds and plants.
- Cultivating peaceful thoughts and words. Remember that violence in the mind will easily spill out of the mouth.
- Keeping company with inspiring, uplifting people who are also working at spiritual growth.
- Maintaining a healthy body. It's hard to be happy and peaceful if the body is weak and sick.

DAY 42

Six Accomplishments

Self-respect is the fruit of discipline; the sense of dignity grows with the ability to say no to oneself.
—Abraham J. Heschel

The Sanskrit word *shatsampatti* means "six accomplishments." These are methods used to evolve spiritually and attain enlightenment. They are often spoken of as "treasures" or "powers" and they are present in every person. The six are:

1. Control of the mind
2. Control of the body
3. Control of desire
4. Control of frustration
5. Control of doubt
6. Control of thoughts

To discover these "treasures" and unearth them requires self-observation and training of mind and body. Here's how to work with these six powers.

- Control the mind by practicing meditation regularly.

- Control the body by doing yoga.
- Control desire by reducing attachment to things and people.
- Control frustration by cultivating patience.
- Control doubt by deepening confidence and trust in yourself.
- Control thoughts by focusing one-pointedly on the present moment. Intentionally cultivating these powers will accelerate your movement toward greater mindfulness.

DAY 43

Lessons From a Legendary Bird

Relationships are like glass. Sometimes it's better to leave them broken than try to hurt yourself trying to put it back together.
—Modern Proverb

Buddhist and Hindu mythology speaks of the hamsa bird, which is much like the swan we see today. There are two unique characteristics of the hamsa. First, it is believed that during the wet, stormy monsoon season, the hamsa flies off to Lake Manasarovar, high up in the Himalaya mountains. It stays there and waits out the monsoons. Secondly, it is said that the hamsa has the ability to drink only the milk out of a mixture of milk and water.

From this, two vital life lessons are developed. Just as the hamsa flies away from the troubles of the monsoons, we too must learn when it's time to move on. And one "time to move on" might show up when a troubled relationship just can't be changed. Moving on is not an act of cowardice. In fact, it may be an act of courage. Even, an act of wisdom. Moving on from a relationship when we have exhausted months or years of effort at repair allows us to focus on relationships that are nurturing and mutually beneficial.

The second lesson of the hamsa concerns its ability to separate milk from water, consuming only the most nutritious part of the mixture. Thus, like the hamsa, it is up to us to extract the good out of all the mixtures of life. If you've been downsized, for example, attempt to see it as an opportunity to consider career options you would normally overlook. If you've been diagnosed with an illness, see it as an opportunity to re-evaluate your lifestyle. If you've been betrayed by a companion or friend, see it as an opportunity to discover what a true friend really is. Life is an enormous mixing pot. It's up to us to extract out of that mixture what is helpful, healthy and will bring us happiness.

DAY 44

When Right Speech Means No Speech

*Pay close attention to what you say—and to why you say it.
When you do, you'll discover that an open mouth
doesn't have to be a mistake.*
—Thanissaro Bhikkhu

Think back to a time—and you probably don't have to go back very far—when you were offended or hurt by what someone said to you. The fact is that our words carry a great deal of power to heal or to hurt, to inspire or to injure. That's why the concept of "right speech" appears on the Buddha's list called the "Eightfold Path." It's number three. This Path simply contains eight ways that combined can lead a person to living a happy, healthy, harmonious life.

In the majority of situations, right speech can mean no speech at all. Here's the way the Buddha elaborated on this view—

- If your words misrepresent the truth in any way, don't speak.
- If your words are divisive, creating rifts between people, don't speak.
- If your words are harsh and will hurt a person, don't speak

- If your words are "small talk" with no purposeful intent, don't speak.

That's the refraining aspect of right speech. On the asserting side, right speech means speaking in ways that are trustworthy, harmonious, healing, comforting, and encouraging. When these positive ways of speaking are offered, then your words become uplifting moments to others.

DAY 45

You Are Divine!

I wish I could show you, when you are lonely or in darkness, the astonishing light of your own being.
—Hafiz

The word "divinity" can be traced back more than 5000 years, originating in Sanskrit where the root *div*—to shine—is found. It refers to that which shines, not only with light but with energy and creativity. This shining is done with its own inherent power not power derived from other sources. Div is often associated with the sun as a symbol because the sun shines with its own light in contrast to the moon which shines only with reflected or borrowed light. This awareness was in the mind of Persian poet Hafiz when he wrote, "I wish I could show you, when you are lonely or in darkness, the astonishing light of your own being."

Shin Buddhists chant *Namu Amida Butsu*, which translates as "I entrust myself to the Buddha of Infinite Light and Life." They do this as a reminder that the same infinite light that emerged from the Buddha exists within themselves. And, among the Buddha's final words was this encouragement: "Be your own light."

What would it take for you to be light—to be divine—for others? A short list would include the following:

- Smile at everyone.
- Listen, really listen and hear what isn't being spoken.
- Compliment people.
- Express appreciation to others.
- Be kinder.
- Be optimistic about everything and everyone.
- Practice generosity in every way you can.

Remember, when you brighten the way for someone else, you also brighten your own path.

DAY 46

Moving Toward Enlightenment

You are here to realize your inner divinity and manifest your innate enlightenment.
—Morihei Ueshiba

The Buddha exhibited great confidence in us by teaching that what he accomplished could be done by any of us. The path to enlightenment isn't all that complicated. Here are five steps:

1. Begin where you are right now and how you are right now.
2. Begin by living morally.
3. Begin by living simply.
4. Begin by meditation—even one or two minutes at a time, to start.
5. Begin by being consistently kind, gentle, compassionate.

Repeat these five steps over and over and over and over . . .

DAY 47

Trusting Yourself

Leap and the net will appear.
—John Burroughs

In Zen circles, John Burroughs' wisdom is often cited: "Leap and the net will appear." Many times, we feel an urge to move our lives into a different direction. For example: to become a yoga teacher; to return to college; to take a creative writing course, but we hesitate and usually hold off by asking ourselves "why." The Burroughs' proverb is a reminder that we don't need to know "why." Just take the step. Respond to that inner wisdom directing you. Let life play its hand out.

Shunryu Suzuki did that. He was a twentieth-century Zen master who lived most of his life in Japan. However, beginning in the 1920s, he wanted to do his work in America. He didn't know any Americans; he had never been to the USA. Yet, the "feeling" never left him. Finally, in 1959, he received an invitation to become the Zen priest at a Japanese American temple in San Francisco. Being a Zen priest wasn't his thing. It involved too much ritual and not enough Zen meditation and teaching. However, he responded because he was mindful of the calling he had felt for decades. He trusted his inner wisdom.

When he arrived in the States, Suzuki was surprised at the high level of interest in meditation and Zen Buddhism expressed by Americans. Soon he was both a Zen temple priest and a Zen meditation teacher. So many Americans began studying with him that the Temple authorities forced him to make a decision: "Be our priest *only* or leave." He left, taking his American students with him. Together, they went on to establish what became the most influential Zen center in the United States—the San Francisco Zen Center. Suzuki Roshi is viewed today as one of the most important Zen teachers of modern times.

He didn't know why he wanted to come here. He didn't need to. He leapt and the net appeared.

You don't need to know why. Leap and the net will appear. Trust your inner wisdom.

DAY 48

Adjusting Is Better Than Complaining

Things are always changing, so nothing can be yours.
— Shunryu Suzuki

Shunryu Suzuki immigrated from Japan to become one of the most influential Zen teachers to Americans. One of his foundational principles was that every routine moment is an opportunity to learn and grow *if we pay attention*. One day, a student asked him why the Japanese made their teacups so thin and delicate that they broke easily. Suzuki's response was that of a true Zen master: "It's not that they're too delicate, but that you don't know how to handle them. You must adjust yourself to the environment and not vice versa."

Too often, most of us are like that student—it's someone else's fault that we're frustrated. In the case of the student who kept dropping and breaking teacups, it's the fault of the Japanese who don't know how to make stronger cups. Suzuki is correct. The student is the source of his own frustration.

The next time you experience frustration, anger, irritation, it can help to offset those by reminding yourself that . . . "No one makes me frustrated; I make myself frustrated. No one makes me angry; I make myself angry.

No one is irritating me; I make myself irritated." In so doing, we adjust ourselves to the environment rather than demanding that life evolves the way we want it to.

DAY 49

Don't Be Yourself—Be a Little Nicer

Treat other lives as your own.
—Sushruta

Sushruta was a 5th century (BCE) Indian physician regarded as the "Father" of surgery and ophthalmology. He advised his students who were studying to be doctors to "treat other lives as your own." His wisdom is applicable to all of us. "Treat other lives as your own" ought to be our daily mantra, spoken when we arise, spoken to ourselves throughout the course of the day.

Perhaps the thought we should awaken to most is that we could be nicer people. This means being nicer to those we love, to those we know well, to those we don't know as well, and to complete strangers. There is an acute shortage of nice people on this planet.

Changing that begins with you. Furthermore, it is neither difficult nor complicated. All it takes is mindfulness. Here some qualities of nice people, qualities which you can adopt and build upon:

- Smile at everyone. Make this a habit.

- Offer sincere compliments. Never pass an opportunity to affirm another person.
- Be polite, more polite than is necessary. (It's always necessary).
- Drop swearing. It's rude, crude, unpleasant to hear and unnecessary.
- Help out. Hold a door open, let a person cut into a line, carry a bag for someone.
- Call people by name. Use his or her name during your conversation. It makes people feel good.
- Give more money. Leave a larger amount in a tip jar. Buy a surprise gift for someone.
- Don't judge. It's definitely not nice.

This list is a mere sampling to get you started. Think how you would like to be treated and then "treat other lives as your own."

DAY 50

Robbing and Replacing

In a mere moment our minds are capable of taking us from heaven to hell and back again.
—Hsing Yun

One of the many stories told about the Buddha and his encounter with people from various walks of life is one about a bandit. The man had robbed from others for decades and came to feel deeply remorseful. Yearning for a better way of living and for a way to transform himself, he approached the Buddha who was teaching in his area. "I am in torment over the suffering I have brought to many people and wish to live differently. Is there a way out of this for me?" the bandit asked.

The Buddha paused and asked: "What are you good at?"

"Nothing!" was the immediate response.

"Nothing? You must be good at something," the Buddha said.

The bandit was silent for a few moments and then said sadly: "The only thing I'm good at is robbing."

"Ah, now we're getting somewhere," said the Buddha. "Robbing is exactly the skill you need to change. I am going to teach you a 'robbing and replacing' meditation. Go and sit quietly somewhere and there rob yourself of all negative thoughts, feelings and emotions. Replace them with positive thoughts, feelings and emotions."

According to the story, the bandit spent twenty-one days in solitude working with the robbing and replacing meditation technique. The legend adds that the bandit became a buddha in his own right, and evolved into a highly regarded and well respected spiritual teacher for the remainder of his life.

Robbing and replacing is a powerful technique for cultivating wisdom and one we can utilize whenever we are feeling discouraged, disappointed or despondent.

DAY 51

Mindfulness Needs Critical Thinking

The mechanical faith which depends on authority and wishes to enjoy the consolations of religion without the labor of being religious is quite different from the religious faith which has its roots in experience.
—S. Radhakrishnan

A story from the East tells of an Indian guru who made his way to a holy river for a purification bath. Many of his devotees and disciples followed him. The guru had very few possessions, but one of them was a small container made from a dried gourd. He used it to collect water from streams and accept food offerings from villagers.

Arriving at the riverbank, he dug a hole in the sand and buried his gourd for safekeeping while he bathed in the holy waters. In order to find it again, he carefully laid a small pile of sand over the location.

The guru's devotees did not see him first bury the gourd, only observing that he made a sand pile near on the riverbank. Assuming this was an important ritual for their teacher prior to wading into the water, they too proceeded to make small piles of sand in the area. When the teacher emerged from his purification rite in the waters, he was astonished to see many sand piles. Of course, he could not find the location of his buried gourd. He asked why his devotees did this. Upon learning that they had imitated him, believing they would gain some spiritual merit, he reprimanded them for their blind faith and foolishness.

Along with teaching mindfulness, the Buddha also stressed the importance of critical thinking. In the Kalama Sutta, which contains teachings of the Buddha emphasizing logic and reason, the Buddha says:

> Do not believe in anything simply because you have heard it. Do not believe in anything simply because it is spoken and rumored by many. Do not believe in anything simply because it is found written in your religious books. Do not believe in anything merely on the authority of your teachers and elders. Do not believe in traditions because they have been handed down for many generations. But after observation and analysis, when you find that anything agrees with reason and is conducive to the good and benefit of one and all, then accept it and live up to it.

Clearly, the Buddha advocates mindfulness and mental skillfulness which employs sound logic and reason. Just as clearly, the Buddha opposes blind faith and the embracing of religious teachings just because they are claimed to be true.

DAY 52

Choosing the Right Friends

You rarely make wise decisions if you surround yourself with fools.
—Rasheed Ogunlaru

The Tirukural is a Tamil scripture which offers guidance about life. One verse cautions about whom we associate with, whom we choose to be our closest friends and companions. It reads: "As water changes according to the soil through which it flows, so a person assimilates the character of his or her associates." (Tirukural 46)

All of us have in our lives people who inspire us as well as those who, in various ways, injure us. This verse from Tirukural is a reminder to ask and respond to these kinds of personal questions:

- Which person/persons do I need to spend more time with?
- Which persons/persons do I need to spend less time with?
- Who are the individuals who lift me up and energize me?
- Who are the individuals who load me up and deplete me?

Of course, the skillful response will be to spend more time with those who lift us up and energize us rather than with those who burden us. Those who are a burden include ones who gossip, who complain constantly, who are negative about everyone and everything, who are drama queens or kings. You know them. Establish a safety zone for yourself from energy vampires.

DAY 53

Letting Your Light Shine

*Darkness cannot drive out darkness: only light can do that.
Hate cannot drive out hate: only love can do that.*
—Martin Luther King, Jr.

Some time ago, an Oakland, California resident was in a hardware store where he was drawn to a two-foot-high Buddha statue. The man was not a Buddhist, nor was he particularly religious. However, he bought the Buddha, returned home and placed the statue on a median strip near his house. The man's hope was that the statue would, in some way, bring a sense of peace and tranquility to a neighborhood marred by crime, drugs, prostitution, garbage and graffiti.

What transpired astonished the man. Soon, area residents began leaving offerings at the base of the Buddha—flowers, fruit, candles. Then, a group of Vietnamese women began to meet regularly in the mornings in front of the statue for group meditation. Little by little, his neighborhood began to change. It became cleaner, quieter and safer. Drug dealers left, prostitutes abandoned the area and crime went down.

In fact, a reporter who heard this account contacted the area police, asking them to check their crime statistics for a block radius around the Buddha statue. They reported that, within two years of the Buddha's appearance, crime dropped by eighty-two percent, robbery reports went from fourteen to three, assaults from five to zero, burglaries from eight to four, drug arrests from three to none and prostitution from three to none.

That story should become a guide, reminding us that a little light can drive away a large darkness. All of us should allow our light to shine in the places where we live and work. When others gossip, we don't. When others are complaining and negative, we continue to be content and positive. A little light can go a long way in our home, on our street and at our place of work.

DAY 54

The Joy of Impermanence

Everything flows and nothing abides, everything gives way and nothing stays fixed.
—Heraclitus

A famous and fascinating Chinese wisdom story is that of a man named Sai Weng who was a horse breeder. One day, his prize horse escaped the fenced area. Upon hearing of his misfortune, a neighbor, feeling badly for Sai Weng, came to console him. However, Sai Weng had a stoical, philosophical attitude about his loss saying: "How could we know this is not a good thing for me?"

A few days later, his prize horse returned with another beautiful horse. This time the same neighbor came over to congratulate Sai Weng on his good fortune. Again, Sai Weng was philosophical saying: "How could we know it is not a bad thing for me?"

After the new horse was trained, Sai Weng's son went out for a ride and broke his leg when he was violently thrown off the horse. His neighbor came by expressing condolences to Sai Weng who simply said: "How could we know it is not a good thing for me?"

Almost a year later, the Emperor's army arrived at the village to conscript all able-bodied men to fight in the war. Because of his injury, Sai Weng's son could not go off to war, and was spared from certain death or serious injury.

This popular Chinese story is about impermanence. It is a reminder that life is constantly changing and fluctuating, from the positive to the negative, from the good to the bad. It teaches us to withhold premature conclusions about an event. We need to allow time to pass and perspective to emerge before we can truly arrive at definitive assessments. The power of this truth is specifically relevant when times are difficult and challenging. It is the concept of impermanence that quietly reminds us that "this too shall pass."

The next time you experience a season of hardship and difficulty, recall the story of Sai Weng. Bring two attitudes to bear upon your challenge: First, bring patience, knowing that things will change. Secondly, bring perspective so that you can look back and see how your burden turned out to contain surprising blessings.

DAY 55

Practicing Self-Care

Most of us are pretty good at keeping promises to others and pretty bad at keeping promises to ourselves.
—Lawrence LeShan

Along with serving others, it is important to perform practices in the service of your own well-being and growth. It's easy to neglect self-care with the result that you can become unhealthy, stressed and burned out. In that condition it's difficult to be of service to others. Here is a simple list of five areas of your life which need to be tended to with regular care:

1. Physical—Are you keeping your body healthy with nutritious food and regular exercise?
2. Intellectual—Are you careful about what goes into your mind being certain that what you read, view, hear is noble and nourishing?
3. Emotional—Are you balanced and not easily thrown off by life's various challenges and changes?
4. Relational—Are you being routinely kind and compassionate to others, being friendly to all?

5. Spiritual—Are you engaging in practices that nourish your spirit and move you toward enlightenment?

Look the list over, assessing which areas need more time and energy from you. Then get to work.

DAY 56

Knowing When to Let Go

*If you let go a little, you will have a little peace.
If you let go a lot, you will have a lot of peace.*
—Ajahn Chah

A man in Thailand was taking his water buffalo out to graze when the animal became frightened by some loud sounds and tried to run away. The rope holding the water buffalo was wound around the man's finger, and when he tried to hold the water buffalo back, the rope tore half his finger off. Screaming in pain and bleeding, the man ran to a nearby monastery with half his finger missing. There, the monks quickly drove him to a clinic for treatment.

He lost a finger not because the water buffalo was frightened and ran, not because the rope was wrapped around his finger. He lost the finger *because he didn't let go.*

There are times in life—many times—when all we need to do is let go. And, when we let go, we can avoid further injury and pain. Furthermore, there are many times in life when we need to let go—let go of the past, let go of a relationship, let go of a job, let go of a career, let go of a child, let go of a loved one.

One image to help us let go is to think of emptying a cup. Intentionally and consciously, work at letting go of your "story"—any inner narrative you constantly repeat to yourself that affirms your victimhood or your rightness. Let it go from your mind, body, heart and spirit. Peace and contentment only come when you let go of the story, empty the cup. Then, new beginnings will open up.

DAY 57

Perfecting Patience

Trees that are slow to grow bear the best fruit.
—Moliere

Taiwanese Buddhist master Hsing Yun tells of taking a group to visit Zen centers in Japan. They exited a train in Tokyo and boarded what they thought was the right bus. After speaking with the driver, however, they learned that it was not. The driver informed them the bus they needed was down a few streets and around a few corners.

Hsing Yun and his group couldn't understand exactly where he was instructing them to go, but there was nothing to do except get off the bus and try to make their way to the correct one. They thanked the driver and stepped out. The bus driver saw the looks of confusion on their faces, turned to the people already sitting on the bus and said: "I am very sorry, but I have to show these people where to catch their bus. Please wait a moment for me. I'll be right back." He turned off the engine, pulled out the keys and jumped down to the street where he guided the group along a very confusing route for about five minutes until they arrived at the correct stop.

A few years later, Hsing Yun returned to Japan to do some teaching. After one of his talks, a young

Japanese man approached him to say hello. He was quite animated and said: "You couldn't possibly remember me, but I remember you. Can you recall a time a few years ago when you were in Tokyo and a bus driver shut off his engine to walk you to your stop? I was one of the passengers on that bus." Hsing Yun remembered and apologized for making all of them wait so long. The young man said that no one minded and, in fact, when the bus driver returned after nearly ten minutes, everyone started clapping their hands in approval of his act of kindness.

There are three important aspects to this story: the first is the driver's kindness in walking the visitors to the bus stop; the second is the support of the driver's kindness by those on the bus; the third is the remarkable patience of those sitting on the bus who waited for his return without complaint.

More of us need to perfect patience.

DAY 58

On Not Making Things Worse

*And oftentimes excusing of a fault
Doth make the fault the worse by the excuse.*
—William Shakespeare

One day, at a Buddhist monastery, ceremonies delayed preparation of the noon meal, which forced the cook to hurry. He took up his sickle and quickly gathered vegetables from the garden, then threw it all into a soup pot, unaware that in his haste he had cut off the head of a snake. At the meal, the monks where highly complementary of the delicious soup, but the Master himself found something odd in his bowl. He summoned the cook and held up the snake head.

"What is this?!?"

The cook responded simply and directly: "Oh, thank you, Master!" the cook said, and immediately ate it.

This is a well-known Zen story titled "Eating the Blame." Here's what's going on in the tale: The cook made a dreadful mistake in not being more mindful. Buddhists are vegetarians and because of his carelessness he made his community a soup out of snake and vegetables. He was clearly at fault, which is why the Master confronted him. However, rather than become defensive and blaming:

"It's your fault for doing such a long ceremony."

"It's your fault for making me hurry to prepare the meal."

"It's the gardener's fault for not keeping snakes out of the garden area."

Instead, he said simply said "Thank you," acknowledging the mistake and swallowed "the blame." Everything was settled quickly, quietly, peacefully and as permanently as possible.

When facing a problem or difficult person, can you respond in ways that don't make it worse?

Far too often when we are confronted with a conflict, we make it worse by becoming defensive, by denying, by arguing, by fighting, etc. When an issue arises, pause and ask yourself, "How can I respond in ways that don't make this worse?"

DAY 59

The Power of an "I Love You"

Feel your love; show your love; speak your love.
—Victor M. Parachin

As the news of a man's diagnosis of terminal cancer spread through his circle of friends, he reported that something unusually pleasant took place. Friends and acquaintances began more freely telling him that they loved him. In turn, he found himself equally freely saying "I love you" to friends and acquaintances. It is truly commendable that his friends responded with love and that he did in return. However, his experiences now raise these questions about saying the three words "I love you":

- Why wait until someone has a terminal illness before saying "I love you"?
- Why are we so timid, hesitant and frightened to say "I love you" to someone outside of the immediate family?
- What is it that holds us back from saying these words, and how can this be overcome?

Everyone wants to be loved but so many feel deprived of love. Why not put onto our lips the love we already feel in our hearts and simply say to our friends "I love you."

Inevitably, when those words are received from someone outside the family there is pleasure, a smile forms, happiness is experience and life becomes joyful in that moment. Don't deprive your friends of those experiences by holding back.

DAY 60

Talk Back to Your Bad Habits

*If you do not pour water on your plant, what will happen?
It will slowly wither and die. Our habits will also slowly wither
and die away if we do not give them an opportunity to manifest.
You need not fight to stop a habit. Just don't give it
an opportunity to repeat itself.*
—Swami Satchidananda

The Tibetan Buddhist teacher Chögyam Trungpa frequently recommended making speeches to our bad habits and negative thoughts. A speech like that can proceed this way: "Judgmentalism—you have brought me nothing but embarrassment and pain. You have caused me far too many problems. I am very sick and tired of you and have decided that I no longer wish to associate with you. Go away because I have absolutely no use for you at all." Or, consider this possibility: "Materialism—you have taken over my life with incessant needs for more and more and more. I am tired of submitting to your endless demands. Now, I want nothing to do with you and am walking away from this relationship with no regrets. Goodbye."

In addition to talking back to bad habits, we can also talk back to our negative thoughts. The most effective way of doing this is by replacing one negative thought with three positive ones. Consider these as some examples for using this technique: "I hate my job" can be supplanted with these three positives: "My job helps me pay my bills. My job lets me donate to worthy causes. My job keeps me off the streets." Or when you find yourself thinking "No one really loves me," supplant that thought with these three: "Though some of my friends may not say 'I love you' directly, their actions reveal their love for me. As I move through my day, I will maintain awareness of love and compassion which comes my way even from strangers. I am a loving person and will make it a point to show and speak love to those around me."

DAY 61

Maintaining a Calm State of Life

Like the ocean that remains calm in its depths even when waves rage over its surface, and like the sun that continues shining on high even during storms, we can at each moment create value and develop our state of life, enjoying our existence to the fullest in times of both suffering and joy.
—Daisaku Ikeda

A man in Los Angeles was pleased to have a mid-week day off from work, so he decided to run some errands and get caught up on things around the house. He enjoyed the opportunity to sleep in later than usual. Deciding to go out, he started his car in the driveway only to remember that he forgot something in the house. Leaving the motor running, he went inside, but when he came back out, his car was gone, vanished. Distraught, he called the police, filed a stolen-auto report and spent the day upset and angry. The joy of having a day off was now filled with frustration over the theft of his vehicle.

However, the next morning, he found his car parked back on his driveway. He went out to inspect the vehicle. It was fine. On the dashboard, he found a white envelope containing a short note. "Sorry to have taken your car but I had an emergency. My child got sick and I had to take him to the hospital. I had no other transportation, so I borrowed your car. As a token of my appreciation, here are two free tickets to the Los Angeles Dodgers baseball game this Saturday."

The man's mood changed toward the very positive as he thought about the incident. His car was returned without damage. His car had been used for a positive purpose. And, he received the gift of two tickets to a professional baseball game.

He and his wife went to the Dodgers game that Saturday, enjoying themselves immensely. When they returned home, they discovered that their house had been burglarized and everything of value had been taken.

That true story is an excellent metaphor reminding us that our lives are constantly changing. There is an ebb and flow between joy and suffering, happiness and sadness, victory and defeat. Often it can change rapidly. One day we have a job, the next day we don't. One day we are healthy, the next day we are sick. The question to consider is: *How do we conduct ourselves* when life constantly moves up and down, through inflation and deflation, through calm and crisis? The tool for dealing with life's constant changes is mindfulness, reminding ourselves of Daisaku Ikeda's wisdom: "We can at each moment create value and develop our state of life, enjoying our existence to the fullest in times of both suffering and joy."

DAY 62

Lessons From a Thief

Most of the shadows in life are caused by standing in our own sunshine.
—Ralph Waldo Emerson

During a December holiday, a teen girl received a card from her uncle with a one-hundred-dollar bill in it. It was the uncle's yearly custom to do this for his niece and nephew. However, this year nothing came in the mail for the nephew. The family waited, believing mail service was slower during the holidays. Several days later, an envelope from the uncle arrived for the nephew. The envelope had been opened and re-sealed. Inside was a twenty-dollar bill. The nephew was confused but thanked his uncle for the twenty dollars. The uncle responded saying, "No, it wasn't twenty, it was a hundred dollars that I put into the holiday card."

The reality that someone stole the boy's holiday gift enraged the family. The father was livid, asking "who steals a child's holiday gift?" The mother, equally frustrated, made comments about the "disgusting lowlifes who don't care." And the grandfather erupted about people who prefer to steal rather than work, saying "there are too many of them." Furthermore, the uncle was scolded for sending cash through the mail in the first place. That entire family had a total meltdown over the incident.

However, in their clouded anger, they missed seeing something significant: the thief had a change of heart. After opening it, the thief didn't just toss away the envelope and card, but returned it to the very house from which it was taken. That act made the thief vulnerable to being discovered. In addition, the thief returned it with some of the money inside. While the wrongness of the theft should not be minimized or glossed over, the entire family did not learn the right lessons from their experience.

Through the modeling by the significant adults in their lives, the children simply saw and learned anger, vengeance and hatred, and missed completely the positive side of the incident: that the thief felt guilt; that the thief returned; that the thief made some restitution; that the thief exhibited compassion and was, perhaps, moving in the direction of self-transformation. What the family lost was greater than the missing holiday cash.

DAY 63

How to Toughen Up

There is nothing that does not grow light through habit and familiarity. Putting up with little cares, I'll train myself to work with great adversity.
—Shantideva

Mithridates VI, known as Mithridates the Great (134-163 BCE) ruled over a large area which is today's Turkey. He was regarded as one of Rome's most formidable and powerful enemies, having engaged and won three major wars against the Roman Empire. His largest threat, however, came from within his own household. His father (Mithridates V) was assassinated when he consumed poison while dining at a lavish palace banquet. Suspecting that the assassin was his mother, Mithridates VI was worried that she would also try to poison him to death. To protect himself, Mithridates began consuming tiny amounts of the various poisons. He did this daily, gradually increasing his dosage. Consequently, he became immune to the common poisons used by assassins of his day.

The experience of Mithridates is a useful way to understand a Buddhist slogan which advises: "Train in the preliminaries." If we learn to appreciate, absorb and accept the small doses of pain which come our way from time to time, then we become stronger for dealing with the larger hardships of life which we encounter later. To toughen up, absorb what comes your way. Deal with it, rather than run from it or avoid it. Learn from it. Keep repeating the pattern. Then you will be trained to work with a greater adversity down the road.

DAY 64

Making Generosity a Habit

The challenge for all of us—adults and children— is to keep that spirit of giving all the time, not just when there is a hurricane, earthquake or tsunami.
—Michelle Singletary

When Maimonides, the great Jewish philosopher and physician, was informed that someone in the community had donated one-thousand gold coins to a person in need he surprised his followers by saying: "It would be much better for the wealthy donor to dispense the one-thousand gold coins one at a time and to one-thousand different recipients."

His point is that too many people give only sporadically, impulsively, inconsistently and usually because they have been moved emotionally to do so. It is much better to give habitually, regularly and consistently. According to Maimonides, the wealthy person could train himself to do this by giving away one gold coin a thousand times to a thousand different people. It's a way of practicing virtue until it comes naturally and becomes an innate part of a person's character.

That ancient wisdom continues to be applicable for us today, making the spirit of giving and generosity a routine habit, so much so that we do it without giving it a second thought.

DAY 65

One Step at a Time

The journey of a thousand miles begins with a single step.
—Lao Tzu

These words of the great Chinese philosopher Lao Tzu may be one of the most powerful and useful ideas ever spoken, one that can be applied to an amazingly diverse range of life issues. For example, an old Tibetan Lama was once asked how he managed to escape from Tibet during the Chinese takeover of his country. The old Lama had walked across the snow-covered Himalayas all the way to safety in India. He had no maps, compasses, weapons, not even tents, sleeping bags or food.

His answer: "I did it one step at a time. Just one step after another."

The next time you face your own "Himalayan Mountain" issue that you need to cross, remember the wisdom of the old Lama and the wisdom of Lao Tzu, that every journey begins with a single step, then another step, and then another step. If you keep taking one step at a time, like the old Lama, you arrive at your destination. It's just that simple!

DAY 66

A Lesson From Zen Master "Bird's Nest"

Slow down. Enjoy this ride. It's all we've got.

—Goldie Hawn

In order to improve their meditation practice, Zen masters often found unusual and even dangerous places to meditate—sitting on a slippery rock in the middle of a river or on the edge of a cliff. Those precarious positions meant being focused, because nodding off could be disastrous. One such Zen master was nicknamed "Bird's Nest Roshi" because he meditated high up on a tree branch in an abandoned eagle's nest. There, one gust of wind or one sleepy moment could result in serious injury or even death. He meditated there to develop and deepen mindfulness and concentration.

As his fame spread, he became a source of both curiosity and criticism. One day, an important government official came to visit him. Standing safely on the ground, he shouted up asking: "Bird's Nest, what possesses you to lie and meditate in such a dangerous manner?"

Bird's Nest responded: "You call this dangerous? What you are doing is far more dangerous!"

What did he mean by that comment?

The Zen master was offering the government official this important lesson: meditation practice develops and strengthens mindfulness. And, the opposite of mindfulness is forgetfulness . . . living unaware . . . living non-attentively. That, to Bird's Nest, was a far more dangerous, disastrous way to live. His comment reflects a similar wisdom from Socrates who said: "The unexamined life is not worth living." So many people rush through their lives never pausing to enjoy the ride. When they realize what they've done, it's too late.

DAY 67

Accepting the Present Moment Fully

> *Mindfulness is the aware, balanced acceptance of the present experience. It is opening to or receiving the present moment, pleasant or unpleasant, just as it is, without either clinging to it or rejecting it.*
> —Sylvia Boorstein

For several weeks, a ninety-two-year-old woman had an unceasing cough. She made several visits to her doctor receiving a variety of diagnoses. Finally, additional testing revealed her lungs were spotted with cancer and she was told she had between two weeks and two months to live.

Returning home, she took time to comprehend this information before sharing the news with her family and friends. Of course, when she informed them there was an outpouring of sadness, distress and advance mourning. However, she herself was amazingly composed and accepting. She explained herself this way:

- "I am ninety-two and have already lived a long, full life."
- "At ninety-two I have no desire to be treated for the cancer."

- "Because I won't be treated, it means I won't suffer any side effects."
- "Knowing this diagnosis gives me time to prepare to die."
- "The short time frame means this will not linger on and on for me."
- "I have good people in my life who will be with me and support me."
- "I'm grateful not to have had cancer in my 40s, 50s, 60s, 70s or 80s."

This ninety-two-year-old woman offers an inspiring example of what it means to truly live in the present moment, not resenting what has come but receiving it with grace, maturity, thoughtfulness and deep wisdom.

DAY 68

Follow Your Bliss

To find your own way is to follow your bliss.
This involves analysis, watching yourself and seeing
where the deep bliss is—not the quick little excitement,
but the real deep life filling bliss.
—Joseph Campbell

The phrase "follow your bliss" has a lot of depth, though the word "bliss" has been misused and abused by a generation of New-Age followers. The word "bliss" is an honored one in Buddhism and in Hinduism. Quite literally, it means extreme happiness and great joy.

Who doesn't want that?

Bliss is a profound concept, one which conveys this life-changing idea: to have bliss in your life, move toward the people and things which bring you extreme happiness and great joy. Conversely, it also means directing your life away from people and things that don't bring you those things and, in fact, bring you their opposites: frustration, disappointment, sadness, fear, anger. That can mean walking away from a family member, friend, a job, a group, a church, a religion, a state, even a country.

A friend of mine decided to follow his bliss saying, "I now have a great life which evokes a tinge of jealousy when it comes up in conversation with some of my friends." He took the time to compile a list of benefits that came by following his bliss. That list includes:

- moving
- falling in love
- going back to school
- starting my own business
- leaving my family's religious traditions and finding my own spiritual path
- traveling the world
- adopting animals
- taking lots of yoga classes
- reading copious amounts of books
- writing
- volunteering
- playing the piano
- making jewelry
- living in an ashram
- buying my dream car

What would it mean for you to follow *your* bliss? Identify it. Then follow it.

DAY 69

Keep a Positive Attitude No Matter What

Choose to be optimistic. It feels better!
—14th Dalai Lama

We've all received such advice as: "Stay positive. Look for the silver lining behind the cloud. See the best in every situation," and so on. But how do you do that when you've experienced a major trauma? Is it realistic and possible to maintain a positive attitude when life has sent a harsh blow? The answer is "yes"!

Here is an inspiring example of someone who did just that. While swimming in the ocean, this man was attacked by a shark. Making it back to the sandy beach, he saw that his left leg was severely damaged. However, his first thought was: "I am the man who conquered a shark." He brought that same positive attitude to his recovery even after learning that his leg injury was so severe that an amputation was necessary. It took six months of rehabilitation and getting used to his prosthetic leg before he could return to work. Rather than drive, which would have placed less pressure on his leg, he opted to do the one-hour commute by train. Commuting meant going up and down several flights of stairs in order to use trains. The man did that because he wanted to strengthen his leg and live as normally as possible.

Sometimes, when standing in front of a mirror, he did "shudder" at what he called his "deformed leg," but immediately another voice reminded him: "It could have been worse. Yes, you lost one leg but you still have a whole other leg. You have two arms. You can walk."

Sometime later, when he learned that a police officer was hit by a car and lost his leg, the man decided to visit the officer in the hospital even though he did not know him. Walking into the policeman's hospital room in his suit, he walked over to the window and placed his leg on the window sill. "I heard about your accident," he said to the man he'd never met. Then he lifted his pants leg and showed the young officer his prosthetic leg. The officer's face lit up and the man said to him: "You're going to be fine!"

In spite of your life's changes and challenges, do stay positive, look for the silver lining behind the clouds and see the best in every situation.

DAY 70

Little Things Make a Big Difference

It has long been an axiom of mine that the little things are infinitely the most important.
—Arthur Conan Doyle

Buddhism teaches that we ought to live in such a way as to be of benefit to others. This is easy to do and simply involves the "little" things of life which actually become "big" things to the receiver.

- Smile.
- Say "please" and "thanks" to everyone.
- Let a car into your lane.
- Allow someone with fewer items to go first in the grocery checkout line.
- Leave tips—generous ones.
- Listen more than you speak.
- Be kinder than is necessary.
- Treat others with respect.
- Give someone the benefit of doubt.
- Don't gossip.
- Encourage friends and strangers.

Make this list much longer by engaging in your unique ways of doing the little things to make a big difference for others.

DAY 71

Mindfully Managing Loss

The sorrow of great and small losses is a river that runs in the underground of all of our lives. When it breaks to the surface, we might feel as though only "I" know this pain. Yet grief is a universal experience.
—Roshi Joan Halifax

"Into each life some rain must fall, some days be dark and dreary," wrote poet Henry Wadsworth Longfellow. Of course, Longfellow is correct in his observation that everyone will experience the presence of sadness and the pain of loss at one time or another—the end of a significant relationship, the death of someone we loved, the loss of health.

Sometimes, the losses come one wave after another. For example, Winston Churchill and his family experienced not merely "some rain" but a torrential downpour, which took place in the span of a few months. In 1921, Churchill and his wife, Clementine, experienced the following losses:

- Clementine's brother—Bill Hozier—ended his life by suicide on April 15 in a Paris hotel room. He shot himself. Both Winston and

Clementine, who were very close to Hozier, were devastated by his death.
- Churchill's mother—Jennie "Lady Randolph"—was only sixty-seven when she fractured her ankle falling down a staircase in her London home. The leg had to be amputated but gangrene set in and she died on June 29th.
- The Churchill's daughter—Marigold, aged two years and nine months—died in her mother's arms on August 23rd from septicemia (a blood infection).
- Earlier in August, Churchill's longtime family friend Thomas Walden died. He first worked for Churchill's father, Lord Randolph, and then for Winston. Walden was very much a member of the Churchill family.

The Churchill family dealt with their losses by taking life one mindful step at a time. Though it was not always easy, the Churchills continued to parent their children, work, entertain, visit friends, deal with their sorrow, and always striving to be of benefit to others. Like the Churchills, everyone who experiences a loss must continue moving mindfully forward in life, doing what needs to done on a daily basis, all while grieving and managing the diverse complexities of grief.

DAY 72

Give Away Some Surprise Money

What we do for others dies with us. What we do for others and the world is immortal and remains.
—Albert Pike

In 1989, the Dalai Lama was awarded the Nobel Peace prize and was asked by reporters how he felt about it. He answered with great humility: "For me personally, nothing special; I am still the same person. But I am really happy for those who had wished me to receive the prize." When another reporter asked what he was going to do with the money, the Dalai Lama looked puzzled and said: "What money?"

Upon being informed that the world's most prestigious award also came with a substantial amount of money, the Dalai Lama immediately responded: "Excellent! I have always wanted to help Baba Amte Colony for lepers in India. Now I can do this!"

His generous act in giving away this gift of "surprise" money is worthy of further consideration on a personal level. When you come into some unexpected income—a tax return, a rebate, a gift from someone—pause to consider ways of sharing it with others rather than simply using it all for your own expenses and pleasures.

DAY 73

Appearances Can Be Deceiving

Your eyes must not determine what you see. Pay attention.
—Mary Anne Radmacher

A spiritually-advanced Tibetan Buddhist teacher tells about an elderly monk who wore tattered clothing and was always hungry. The old monk made it a point to walk through the villages precisely at mealtimes so that villagers would take note of him and make him offerings of food, clothing and even money. Whenever the Tibetan teacher was invited to give a teaching before a large group, the elderly, ragged monk asked to accompany him, knowing that the Tibetan's supporters would make offerings to everyone who came with him.

At one of those occasions, the elderly monk died. The Tibetan teacher and some of his followers went to the modest home of the monk. There, they found that he had been sleeping on seven-hundred silver coins. At the time, those coins were worth a great deal of money in Tibet. The teacher and his party were astonished because they always thought the man was very poor.

Then, one of those present noticed what appeared to be a fake wall and suggested that there might be more money behind it. The group carefully broke into the wall and found several more bags of silver coins. Each bag was so heavy that it was almost impossible for two men to lift. Again, those present were stunned as they realized that most of the people who fed and supported that elderly monk were far poorer than he was.

This incident serves as a clear reminder that appearances can be very, very deceiving.

Just because someone is a Buddhist monk, even dressed in robes, does not mean he or she is an enlightened being who should be blindly followed and supported. Just because someone appears to be successful may not mean that his or her personal and professional life is not in shambles. Just because someone appears to be honest and virtuous does not mean that the person operates that way "behind the scenes."

While it is difficult not to be deceived by appearances, one way of dealing more effectively with appearance is *awareness*—such as by simply paying attention and noticing when "cracks in the veneer" appear, times when a person's actions and explanations indicate that something is amiss. At those moments, pause and evaluate carefully whether or not the relationship should proceed.

DAY 74

Courage to Take a Stand

People deal too much with the negative, with what is wrong. Why not try and see positive things, to just touch those things and make them bloom.
—Thich Nhat Hanh

If you have ever been criticized in public you know how hurtful, how humiliating it feels, and how long the pain can linger. That may have been one of the reasons why Swami Sivananda (1887-1963) took time to write a letter of reprimand to one of his students. That student had written and published a pamphlet criticizing the founder of a prominent ashram nearby. Here are excerpts from Swami Sivananda's admonition to his student:

> I have come to know that you have published a small pamphlet wherein you have indirectly attacked an Ashram in Punjab. You ought not to have done this. It is vilification. It is not a noble act for a Sannyasi (a spiritual ascetic and teacher). Petty minded householders will only behave like this. In the future don't do anything of this kind. You are still very weak. You are swayed or tossed by words. "Tit for tat" is the nature of householders not Sannyasins. To bear

insult and injury is the nature of Sannyasins. That is spiritual strength. That is balance. To be moved by trifles, to waste energy in a useless direction is not wisdom.

Swami Sivananda concludes his letter of reprimand instructing his student to

> ... keep quiet. Stop selling the remaining copies of the pamphlet and destroy them. Keep the mind cool and direct your attention to meditation and other useful work. This affair is serious. I want you to keep absolute silence in the future.

It was commendable and courageous of Swami Sivananda to correct the critic. Too many people place too much focus on being negative, critical, unkind, mean-spirited. It's not a good way to live and it's not good for other people. More responses like that of Swami Sivananda are needed, as are more people who stand ready to correct a critic and possibly inspire them to rein in their unpleasant conduct.

DAY 75

Lean Into the Sharp Points of Life

We grow more quickly if we are open to working with difficulties rather than constantly running away from them.
—Traleg Kyabgon

An important teaching that comes from Tibetan Buddhism is the phrase "lean into the sharp points." The phrase simply means that wise individuals will use, for noble purposes, anything that provokes resentment or anger.

One way of doing this is provided by Chögyam Trungpa, one of the most influential Tibetan Buddhist teachers in the West. At one time, he became the target of personal criticism coming from several directions. Upon learning of this, he immediately began to repeat this affirmation for his critics:

> May whoever has contact with me and my lineage receive its blessing and make an auspicious connection. May whoever hurls harsh words or even stones at me, hit me and thus make an auspicious connection. May my life be beneficial to all beings.

His example shows a more beneficial and more useful way of responding to the negative that comes our way. Too often we choose only from the following options: surrender, withdrawal or counterattack. However, there is another option: leaning into it, facing it, looking at it, studying it and then responding, not reacting, in a skillful, mature, wise, growth-promoting way.

DAY 76

Sometimes a Touch Is More Powerful Than a Word

Too often we underestimate the power of a touch, a smile, a kind word...all of which have the potential to turn a life around.
—Leo Buscaglia

When the Dalai Lama was participating in a seminar in Long Beach, California, a small group of people often waited outside the home where he was hosted. One afternoon, as the Dalai Lama returned to the house, a visibly disturbed man shouted out at him.

Going over to the man, the Dalai Lama patiently listened as the man ranted about the pointlessness of his life and existence. When the man was through, the Dalai Lama gently suggested that he focus on the good things in his life, the importance of his presence in the lives of his loved ones and the many good things he could do with his life by helping others.

When it became obvious that the man could not or would not hear this wisdom, the Dalai Lama gave up talking and simply gave him a big bear-hug. As the Dalai Lama held him, the man sobbed loudly, then became calm and relaxed.

We must never forget that there are times when careful listening and responding with a touch or an embrace are much more powerful and healing than our words.

DAY 77

Be an Agent of Change

*Don't believe the lie that you can't change the world.
You can and you are not alone.*
—Victor M. Parachin

Several years ago, a global conference on social justice and change was held in Hiroshima, Japan. Three Nobel Peace Prize winners were among the speakers: Bishop Desmond Tutu of South Africa, Betty Williams of Northern Ireland and the 14th Dalai Lama. During a question and answer period with the three global leaders, a young woman from Mexico spoke passionately through tears over her frustration that the United States was building a wall along the Mexican-US border in order to keep out people from Mexico.

Ms. Williams sent an assistant to simply embrace the young woman. Bishop Tutu offered words of encouragement based on his own experiences resisting South Africa's apartheid policies. The Dalai Lama shared with her the view of engaged Buddhism and the importance of self-confidence: "You have to work," he advised. "There are thousands of people who will help you. You are never alone. But the main work is on your own shoulders. You should not lose hope. You should be optimistic and have self-confidence."

It's a myth and a lie that one person can't change the world. Right before her eyes that young Mexican woman could see three individuals who did just that: a mother and homemaker from Northern Ireland who acted against the violence in her country; a black man from South Africa who resisted apartheid; and a Tibetan-in-exile challenging the Chinese persecution of Tibetan Buddhists.

DAY 78

Compassion Is Contagious

Why not do your part to spread the "virus" of compassion?
—Victor M. Parachin

High in the Himalayan mountains, a Tibetan Buddhist monk rescued an old German Shepherd dog that was going to be killed. He gave the dog his walled-in garden area, carefully looking after his needs and feeding him properly.

Then one day, an injured or sick baby rabbit made its way into the garden, quite weak and exhausted. Amazingly, the German Shepherd licked, cleaned and nuzzled the little rabbit. This was amazing because the normal tendency of most dogs would be to kill small creatures.

What explains this unusual conduct? Perhaps this, and it's an important lesson from the animal world—compassion is contagious. The Tibetan monk was kind and compassionate to the dog and now the dog was being kind and compassionate to another creature.

This principle applies to the world of humans as well. By simply being a nicer person and by merely treating others with kindness, we have the power to empower others to do the same as they move forward in their day.

Experiment with this yourself. As you go through your day, be intentional about making eye contact with individuals, smile at them, exude a pleasant, positive attitude toward each one. Furthermore, if you are in a routine conversation with people, such as ordering a coffee or making a purchase, add to your smile a sincere compliment about the individual.

You'll make *their* day, and, in turn, they will make someone else's day. Catholic Sister Thea Bowman wisely observed: "Sometimes people think they have to do big things in order to make change. But if each one would light a candle we'd have a tremendous light."

DAY 79

Avoid Rushing Toward Enlightenment

Those who are in a hurry to become enlightened are like caterpillars rushing out of their cocoons to become butterflies. Their haste ensures that they will either die in the process or be killed by predators.
—Sheng Yen

A friend of mine is a martial arts teacher. He once told me that he turns away every potential student who first asks, "How long will it take me to get a black belt in Karate?" That question, he explained, indicates someone who simply wants instant results, and who is unwilling to expend the time, discipline and effort necessary to achieve the goal.

That's the idea conveyed in the quote by Chinese Zen master Sheng Yen when he talks about "those who are in a hurry to become enlightened." There are many who rush to enlightenment and then "die" in the process.

We've all come across such individuals—the alcoholic who attends three or four recovery group meetings before dropping off; someone diagnosed with a mental illness who quits taking his medication saying, "I don't need them anymore"; a woman in marriage-therapy who terminates the sessions because "it's too painful"; a man who registers for a series of classes on meditation but stops attending even before the course is over; the person who joins a gym and exercises for a few weeks and then is never seen there again; the recreational jogger who decides to run a marathon but fails to train consistently.

Enlightenment in any endeavor requires the commitments of patience, perseverance and persistence for true progress to be experienced.

DAY 80

Cultivate Wisdom

We can't simply study and swiftly acquire wisdom, but we can gradually become wise. And we must do so not only for our own sake but also for the sake of everyone else in this sorely troubled world.
—Lama Surya Das

The art of being wise is noticeably and painfully absent in our modern era. This was likely also the case in the Buddha's time. Thus, Buddhism not only promotes wisdom but offers five ways of gaining wisdom.

1. Wisdom gained through **silence.** Meditation is the first tool to use in acquiring wisdom. This was one of the earliest utterances of the Buddha: "Meditation brings wisdom; lack of mediation leaves ignorance. Know well what leads you forward and what holds you back and choose the path that leads to wisdom."
2. Wisdom gained through **listening.** This means listening to teachers of Buddhism and other wisdom traditions. This listening can be in the form of attending regular *dharma* talks, attending retreats where teachings are offered, reading books, listening to podcasts, attending on-line

courses, and watching videos that explain teachings.
3. Wisdom gained through **thinking.** After listening to teachings, one must reflect on those teachings and process them internally. Otherwise, the teachings will not be remembered and do no good. Learning wisdom is only possible by deeply considering these teachings.
4. Wisdom gained through **practice.** The words must be turned outward and into action. One grows into wisdom through an ever-present observation of one's thoughts, words and deeds, constantly adjusting them to align closely to the wisdom of the inner buddha.
5. Wisdom gained through **teaching** others. One learns more by teaching others. Wisdom can be solidified as one shares and teaches wisdom. Doing this forces the mind to review what it has already learned and reinforces it in memory.

DAY 81

Become a More Tolerant Person

Know thy neighbor. We can never know how other people live. Such a lack of experience makes for intolerance.
—K. Sri. Dhammananda

The most direct route to becoming a more tolerant person is by getting to know people who are not like you.

If you are a healthy person, it's almost impossible to know what it's like to be chronically ill. Get to know someone who struggles with an illness.

If you are one whose energy is consistently strong, it will be difficult for you to understand someone whose energy limits their activities. Get to know someone with consistently low energy.

If you're a white American, you are automatically getting privileges and opportunities not as readily available to people of color. Consequently, it's impossible to understand racism when you have white privilege. Get to know someone whose skin color isn't white.

You can add to this list . . .

- If you're a male...
- If you're wealthy...
- If you have many friends ...

- If you are highly educated…
- If you have a great, fulfilling job…
- If you have a beautiful home with a spacious yard ….

DAY 82

Sun Faced Buddha, Moon Faced Buddha

Grumble, if your nature calls you to it, but persevere.
—Sri Aurobindo

When it comes to a meditation practice, most people will do fine by participating in a meditation group. However, it's a little tougher to keep a personal home practice going.

This was as true in past centuries as it is today, which is why one ancient Chinese Zen master offered this simple statement to motivate students who were becoming sluggish about meditation, "Sun Faced Buddha, Moon Faced Buddha!"

By those words he meant that meditation should be done when happy or sad, energetic or tired, healthy or ill. "Just do it" was his advice.

Actually, "Sun Faced Buddha, Moon Faced Buddha" can apply to other areas of life, such as studying, exercising, cleaning the house or maintaining your yard. Whenever you "don't feel like it" remind yourself of the Zen master's wisdom and say to yourself, "Sun Faced Buddha, Moon Faced Buddha."

DAY 83

Red Light Meditation

The next time you are caught in traffic, don't fight. It is useless to fight. If you sit back and smile to yourself, you will enjoy the present moment and make everyone in the car happy.
—Thich Nhat Hanh

Driving along a major street recently, I seemed to connect with every single red light. I found myself irritated. Then, I realized there's a better way to deal with red lights (and stop signs as well). Treat each red light as a friend who . . .

- is a reminder to be in the present moment
- is a reminder to be more mindful
- is a reminder to smile
- is a reminder to take a few deep breaths
- is a reminder that it's there to keep people safe
- is a reminder to sit in silent meditation
- is a reminder to chant OM
- is a reminder to send lovingkindness to a friend dealing with a tough issue
- is a reminder to pause and ask, "What's the rush, really?"

Doing this will ensure a much more relaxing car ride, will make you happier, and will "make everyone in the car happy."

DAY 84

Collecting Good Karma

We need to create circumstances conducive to our development. Since we live in a world that is created by and operates through karma, we have to abide by its laws and travel the path of positive karma.
—Tulku Thondup

Karma literally means an act or an action. The essence of karma is simple: that one's life will be better if one acts in ways that are ethical and it will be worse if one acts in ways that are unethical. If an action taken is positive, there will be a positive result. If an action taken is negative, there will be a negative response. The concept of karma means that we alone are ultimately responsible for our lives.

Furthermore, there is this important distinction about karma: every human action produces a consequence, *but* the law of karma does not hold that every action experienced is a consequence. Karma is not fatalistic.

In addition, the scales of karmic justice favor humanity—when a person generates an ounce of virtuous karma, the Universe (or God) increases it significantly returning to the person four or five ounces of benefit. One's good karma has a unique power in that it is able to increase itself, while the negative karma stays just as it is. This philosophy inspires hope and confidence that, regardless of negative acts and karmas, positive ones will eventually outweigh them.

Here is an excellent method for collecting good karma daily. Each evening before falling asleep, ask yourself "Where during the day did I collect good karma? Did I assist someone, reduce anger in myself or another person, avoid an argument, speak kindly, help an animal?" Hopefully, there will be "yes" answers to the questions, but if not, simply commit to intentionally collect good karma the next day.

DAY 85

Mind Cleansing

I don't envision a single thing that, when undeveloped, leads to such great harm as the mind. The mind, when undeveloped, leads to great harm. I don't envision a single thing that, when developed, leads to such great benefit as the mind. The mind, when developed, leads to great benefit.
—Buddha

It is a well-known Buddhist teaching that we are what we think. What's less well known is that the Buddha also offered this four-step process for cleansing the mind:

1. to discard unhealthy thoughts that have taken residence in the mind
2. to eliminate unhealthy thoughts as soon as they appear
3. to nurture healthy thoughts that appear by putting them into daily practice
4. to cultivate healthy thoughts that have not yet emerged.

Allow the Buddha's four-step mind-cleansing process to work for you by taking a daily inventory of what's in your mind and follow his pattern—discard, eliminate, nurture, cultivate.

DAY 86

The "Maharishi" Effect

Never underestimate the power of a small group of committed people to change the world. In fact it is the only thing that ever has.
—Margaret Mead

There is community benefit in meditation as well as the well-known personal benefits. An experiment was done in Merseyside, England, to test something called the "Maharishi" effect. Named after Eastern teacher and guru to the Beatles, Maharishi Mahesh Yogi, who said that if one percent of a population meditated daily for a prolonged period of time, the effect on a community could be measured and would be positive.

Working with residents of Merseyside, researchers were able to enroll more than one percent of the population to meditate together every day from 1988 to 1991. The result was astonishing as the crime rate dropped so much that Merseyside went from the third highest to the lowest-ranked city in England during the time of the analysis.

Meanwhile, in the control group, a town of non-meditators, the crime rate held steady. Meditation was the only factor in the study that could account for the change, as the scientists calculated that police practices, local economics and demographics remained the same throughout the study.

Two ideas emerge from this fascinating experiment. First, meditation is important and, of course, meditation can be done alone in the comfort and privacy of our personal environment. But, secondly, group meditation is also important. In a group, not only are we supported by like-minded people, but in meeting together regularly there is a ripple effect that brings peacefulness into the surrounding community.

DAY 87

Suspending Judgment

The skillful mind does not rush to judgment assessing what is good and what is bad, what is favorable and what is unfavorable.
—Victor M. Parachin

One of the most beloved and influential individuals in Jewish history is Rabbi Akiva (c. 40—137 CE). This highly regarded Torah scholar was walking one day accompanied by a rooster and a donkey and carrying a lamp. Arriving at a small village, he sought refuge for the night, but the only inn was full. So, with his lamp, his donkey and his rooster, he retired to a field nearby where they settled in to spend the night sleeping outdoors.

That evening, a strong, loud windstorm emerged and blew out his lamp. Because of the noisy winds, Rabbi Akiva did not hear it when a fox came and ate his rooster. Nor did he hear a mountain lion approach and devour his donkey. Of course, the losses of his beloved creatures were upsetting, yet he adhered to his philosophy that things happen for a reason and, in the end, "it's all good."

During that same night while he slept in the open field, a mercenary army attacked the village killing those who resisted and capturing all others to sell off as slaves. Learning of this, he immediately realized that, had the rooster crowed, had the donkey brayed, had his light glowed, he would have been discovered, possibly killed and certainly carried off as a slave.

The message from that experience is important. We must not rush to judgment, concluding an event to be bad, negative, devastating. Rather, we must suspend coming to definitive conclusions because the story is not complete. It's important to refrain, hold back and wait for the larger picture to emerge. Only with the passing of time can we properly evaluate the full meaning of an event or experience.

DAY 88

You Are the Light of Your World!

*When you share your light with others,
your own light is not diminished, rather
your light expands, extends, and extinguishes
the darkness.*
—Victor M. Parachin

This planet is waiting for people to heal it. More specifically, this world needs you to bring it hope and healing. The Buddha famously said that "thousands of candles can be lit from a single candle, and the life of that candle will not be shortened." Too many people feel powerless and, therefore, hopeless about making a difference. Yet, think about a dark room. When even one candle is lit some illumination enters the space. When that same candle is used to light another candle and then another and another, the illumination is expanded greatly. If you, as the candle, continue to light many other candles, the darkness will give way to a brilliant illumination.

> Be a candle in your small part of the planet—
> Where there is despair, be a candle of hope.
> Where there is indifference, be a candle of love.
> Where there is hatred, be a candle of compassion.
> Where there is ill-will, be a candle of good-will.

Where there is injustice, be a candle of justice.
Where there is sorrow, be a candle of comfort.

Remember, when you share your light with others, your own light is not diminished. Rather, your light expands and extends and extinguishes the darkness. You are the light of your world!

DAY 89

Having an Unflappable Mind

The power of the mind is in itself neither positive nor negative—it just is! It can work both ways depending where it is directed.
—Indra Devi

In the Zen Buddhist tradition there is a popular story of two monks standing outside near a flagpole and enjoying the weather. Looking at the flagpole, one monk said to the other: "See how the flag moves in the wind." The other monk corrected him: "No, a flag can't move. It is the wind that is moving." Overhearing their conversation, the Zen master corrected both monks: "Neither the flag nor the wind is moving. Mind is moving." As the story goes, upon hearing the Zen master's wisdom, the two monks gained a new insight into the nature of mind.

That insight was this: Life is constantly changing, shifting, reshaping. Nothing remains the same for very long. The Buddhists call this the principle of impermanence. Therefore, it is important to have a mind that is "unflappable" in order to remain strong, stable and secure.

Another Zen story illustrates this principle powerfully. Centuries ago, a Korean Zen master traveled to

China in order to teach Zen Buddhism. The boat he sailed on also carried a group of convicts. Somehow, that Zen master was mistaken for one of the prisoners and brought before a judge. All he could say in his defense was that he was a Buddhist monk, not a criminal. The magistrate did not believe him and sentenced him with the others. Upon hearing this, the monk did not protest. Rather, he simply and calmly sat there using the opportunity for meditation.

Next, the judge decided to have thirty of the prisoners executed as an example to everyone else and to serve as a deterrent. The Zen master was included among the thirty to receive the death penalty. As he waited for his turn to be executed, he continued to be calm and remained in meditation. This caught the attention of the judge who found his quiet, peaceful demeanor unusual. "Who *are* you?" the judge asked him. Again, the Zen master said he was a Buddhist monk. This time the judge believed him and ordered him released.

Those who reported this incident said that, when the Zen master was first arrested he did not exhibit fear, anger or panic, and when he was released he didn't seem particularly excited and overjoyed. He simply continued on to his destination.

This is an example of having an "unflappable" mind. Certainly, the situation faced by the monk was extreme and one we would likely not find ourselves in. However, his example can remind us to maintain a balanced approach to life, especially when it gets rough. Rather than react wildly we can choose to respond thoughtfully and skillfully.

DAY 90

Living With No Regrets

*From the many life options, choose your path wisely.
Then follow that path without vacillating.*
—Victor M. Parachin

According to hospice workers—those who care for people at the time of death—the five biggest regrets of dying people are:

1. wishing not to have worked so hard
2. to have had courage to express feelings, especially those of affection
3. to have stayed in touch with friends
4. to have let oneself be happier.

But the fifth one was, by far, the largest life disappointment—the lack of courage to live true to oneself rather than living the life others expected.

The time to avoid this fifth regret is starting now. Some ways of doing that include: 1) become aware of the issue and minimize it, 2) work hard *and* leave room for life's pleasures, 3) express feelings of affection to those around you, 4) stay in touch with your friends, 5) let yourself be happier, and 6) pursue your passions rather than doing what others expect of you.

It's important to learn to live well in order to experience satisfaction and fulfillment in life. If we don't learn to live, then we simply end up fidgeting until death.

DAY 91

Practice Versus Profession

> *Belief must be reinforced by behavior and creeds must be matched by deeds.*
> —Victor M. Parachin

Professing a path is good. Practicing the path is better. Of course, ideally, profession is always backed up by practice. However, the reality is that all too often what one believes is not supported by one's behavior.

One who exemplified his practice of Buddhism powerfully was a Zen monk named Tetsugen Doko (1630-1682). Along with teaching Buddhism, a great desire of his life was to publish an important Buddhist sutra (scripture) in Japanese so that the common person could read the Buddha's teachings for themselves. He began traveling all over Japan to raise money for the publication. It took him ten years to collect enough money to hire someone to make the woodblocks for the printing.

Just as he was about to make the final arrangements for publication, parts of Japan experienced severe flooding. Many people lost their homes and all of their belongings. Tetsugen took the money he had collected for nearly a decade and gave it to homeless families so they could rebuild. After that, he started fundraising for his project a second time. Again, after traveling across Japan for ten years he collected the necessary funds for publication. Right at this time, an intense period of drought afflicted Japanese farmers. Little food was grown and people were starving to death. Once more, Tetsugen took the publication money he had raised and purchased large quantities of rice for the people.

As soon as those needs were met and when life returned to normal, Tetsugen again began criss- crossing the country, often on foot, to raise money for the publication of the Buddhist sutra. This third time he managed to get it printed. As the Japanese people learned of his thirty-year effort, they honored Tetsugen by telling their children his story saying: "The monk Tetsugen actually produced three printings of the sutra, but of these three the first two were the most important."

It was Tetsugen's practice of Buddhism that had far more impact than his mere profession of the way.

DAY 92

Living a Better Life

The only real failure in life is not to be true to the best one knows.
—Buddha

To live a good life and die a good death, do what Buddhists have traditionally done—meditate on the following realities summed up in five sentences:

1. I am of the nature to age, I have not gone beyond aging.
2. I am of the nature to sicken, I have not gone beyond sickness.
3. I am subjected to my own karma, I am not free from karmic effects.
4. I am of the nature to die, I have not gone beyond dying.
5. All that is mine, beloved and pleasing, will change, will become otherwise, will become separated from me.

Though this contemplation on aging, sickness, change and death may initially appear negative and unpleasant, Buddhism teaches that it brings these three benefits:

1. freedom from fear of aging, of sickness, of death
2. a new vision of living and, with it, a better focus of values
3. an empowerment to die with dignity, not with fear and regret.

DAY 93

Be Your Own Witness

You should be your own witness. Don't take others as your witness. This means learning to trust yourself.
—Ajahn Chah

A witness is someone who speaks to the truth or accuracy of an event or circumstance. However, many times, witnesses are not reliable transmitters of reality. That's why there is great wisdom in Ajahn Chah's advice: "Be your own witness. Don't take others as your witness. This means trusting yourself."

I have a friend who was studying at a community college, planning to become a doctor. While doing research about courses to take in preparation for medical school, she learned that it was possible to be admitted into med school after three years of undergraduate study and without completing a degree. She decided to try that route, which meant studying for the medical school entrance exam, volunteering many hours at a local hospital, and continuing her community college courses.

Immediately, everyone around her told my friend it was impossible to get into any medical school without completing an undergraduate degree. She disregarded her "witnesses" and continued this path. Before her twenty-first birthday and while in her third year of college, she was accepted directly into medical school. Furthermore, after she completed her first year of med school, her college awarded her an undergraduate degree based on her medical school classes. She will be one of the youngest to graduate with an MD degree.

Clearly, this is a young woman who knows how to trust herself and be her own witness. She is able to make decisions based on her understanding of situations, not relying upon the understanding of other people. This gives her a great deal of life freedom and continually strengthens her self-confidence.

DAY 94

Four Tips for Living a Buddhist Life

When one does what Buddhas do, one is a Buddha.
—Hsuan Hua

Growth, whether it's intellectual or spiritual, personal or professional, involves intention and commitment. Here are four tips for living a more effective Buddhist life.

1. *Do good.* In Buddhist terms this is called "gathering merit." It means cultivating and maintaining the wish to be of benefit to all beings in all the ways you can and in all the places you can. Do good based upon honorable intentions, pure motives and a sincere desire to help.
2. *Seek role models.* Essentially, a guru is simply a great role model. Do your research and identify persons, living or deceased, who you can look up to and emulate. My own role models are teachers from earlier times whose writings and lifestyles have made a positive impression upon me—Patrul Rinpoche, Shantideva, Swami Vivekananda and Swami Sivananda.
3. *Use intelligent compassion not "idiot compassion."* For compassion to be effective it has to be applied wisely, skillfully and with intelligence. Without

those ingredients, we can end up supporting an unhealthy habit or unwholesome practice. For example, feeding your animal companion every time it pleads for food can result in obesity. "Idiot compassion" (a phrase coined by the Tibetan master, Chögyam Trungpa Rinpoche) offers it food; intelligent compassion regulates how much and how often it is fed.

4. *Cultivate self-confidence.* This is vital because all of us will experience setback, disappointment and failure. When these unwelcome moments occur, it's easy to lose our dignity and confidence. It is crucial that we continue to remain focused, unswerving, determined to continue moving forward. Cultivate self-confidence. It is an effective antidote to discouragement.

DAY 95

Two Powerful Tools for Dealing with Life

The secret for both body and mind is not to mourn for the past, not to worry about the future, or not to anticipate troubles, but to live in the present moment wisely and earnestly.
—Buddha

There is no such thing as a stress-free life and there are no people who live without anxieties and concerns. Take advantage of utilizing two powerful tools for dealing skillfully with whatever comes your way in life.

The first tool is yoga. This ancient health science was used by the Buddha to steady his body so that he could work more effectively with his mind. Find a yoga studio and join with others to experience the physical, emotional, mental and spiritual benefits of this practice. The word "yoga" comes from the Sanskrit term *yuj* and literally means "join together" or "unify." Yoga enables us to tap into our three inner healers: our inner physician to heal the body; our inner psychiatrist to heal the mind; our inner priest to heal the soul.

The second tool is meditation. Don't fall for the seductive lie that you don't have time for it or that it's too complicated. Meditation is something anyone can do and everyone can benefit from. If you don't know where to start here are three suggestions:

1. Get a book or two from the library and read about meditation.
2. Find a meditation group in your community and begin attending regularly.
3. Find a meditation style that resonates with you and start using it several times a week.

Before long, you'll find yourself becoming more focused and less scattered, more compassionate and less frustrated.

It's important to work with both yoga and meditation, because together they create a powerful energy for living in the present moment "wisely and earnestly."

DAY 96

Buddhism and War

*All fear violence, all are afraid of death.
Seeing the similarity to oneself, one should
not use violence or have it used.*
—Buddha

At its very core, Buddhism is all about non-violence. The Sanskrit word is *ahimsa* and this concept permeates Buddhist thought (as well as Hindu philosophy). The first of the five precepts of Buddhism, to which one must adhere as a Buddhist, states simply and clearly: "Do not kill" or "Abstain from harming living beings."

That this philosophy is vital, appears in an encounter Vietnamese Buddhist monk Thich Nhat Hanh had with an angry war veteran who was rebuking Nhat Hanh about his unswerving dedication to non-violence.

"You're a fool," said the veteran. "What if someone had wiped out all the Buddhists in the world and you were the last one left. Would you not try to kill the person who was trying to kill you, and in doing so save Buddhism?!"

Thich Nhat Hanh answered patiently:

> It would be better to let him kill me. If there
> is any truth to Buddhism and the Dharma, it

will not disappear from the face of the earth but will reappear when seekers of truth are ready to rediscover it.

In killing, I would be betraying and abandoning the very teachings I would be seeking to preserve. So, it would be better to let him kill me and remain true to the spirit of the Dharma.

DAY 97

Meditation "Therapy"

It is important to stop in time and look at one's past up until this moment, to look closely at the person we have been so far.
—Akira Ishii

Sometimes one feels disconnected from life and from others. There can be a variety of reasons for this, but a highly effective way of restoring that link is to practice a form of meditation "therapy" called *Naikan*, which is the Japanese word for "looking inside." Naikan meditation therapy was developed by Ishin Yoshimoto (1916-1988), a Japanese Buddhist layperson. As a young man, he spent a great deal of time in meditation, specifically looking inside himself. He found deep insight so helpful and powerful for his daily life that he began introducing it to people in Japan during the 1940s.

Since then it has spread worldwide and helps people better understand themselves, their actions, their relationships and broadens their view of reality. It is used in mental health counseling, addiction treatment and the rehabilitation of prisoners. Though powerful, it is relatively simple, involving three sentences for meditation focus. Here's how it's done:

Bring to your mind an individual. This could be a parent, relative, friend, colleague, your husband, wife, boyfriend, girlfriend. The person can be living or deceased, someone from your distant past or someone very present. Think about that person and ask yourself these three questions taking your time to reflect carefully on each one:

1. What have I received from this person?
2. What have I given to this person?
3. What troubles and difficulties have I caused for this person?

Ideally, Naikan meditation therapy ought to be done on a daily basis or at least several times a week, looking back over the previous hours or days, carefully assessing ourselves and our interactions with others. Ten to thirty minutes is all that it takes. This simple meditation process is powerful for three reasons:

1. It increases our awareness of pleasures that come from others (question #1).
2. It brings our attention to the fact that we can and do act generously, kindly toward others (question #2).
3. It awakens us to ways that we inconvenience others or cause them problems.

Engaging in this practice reduces our all-too-human tendency to live out a self-edited, narrow version of our lives.

DAY 98

Eating Mindfully

When we are mindful, we recognize what we are picking up. When we put it into our mouth, we know what we are putting into our mouth. When we chew it, we know what we are chewing. It's very simple.
—Thich Nhat Hanh

Chan Khong is a Buddhist nun and peace activist who conducts retreats worldwide and works closely with Vietnamese Zen teacher Thich Nhat Hanh. She grew up in a family that included twenty-two children. Her parents had nine of their own children along with twelve nieces and nephews who lived with them while they attended school. In addition, the parents also took in one girl from a poor village family. Chan Khong says that, in spite of the large number of children in the household, each child was properly fed, clothed, educated and treated with equal kindness and consideration by her parents.

Because the family was so large, there was a shortage of food, but everyone learned to be satisfied and to share what was available. Chan Khong recalls that every morning each child was given one Vietnamese *dong* to buy a sweet potato for breakfast from one of the schoolyard vendors. Lunch consisted of a small bowl of rice, soy sauce and one boiled egg. Chan Khong always ate the rice with soy but saved the boiled egg for the afternoon recess. At that time, she ate it very slowly. First the white, carefully taking off one piece at a time and dipping it into a mixture of salt and pepper. Then she did the same with the yellow yolk. She was able to eat so slowly and mindfully that the one egg lasted the entire fifteen-minute break. When she peeled away all the white and the yolk appeared, she always experienced it as a beautiful sunrise.

When Chan Khong came to the West she was astonished and dismayed by how people took an egg for granted. As a result, she often teaches her Western friends a "boiled-egg-appreciation" meditation. Perhaps this is something we ought to do periodically, not only with a boiled egg but with the food that is before us. Pause to appreciate what we have; eat what is before us slowly, mindfully, intentionally and with great gratitude.

DAY 99

Thoughts About Death

*According to the Buddhist way of thinking, death,
far from being a subject to be shunned and avoided,
is the key that unlocks the seeming mystery of life.
It is by understanding death that we understand life.*
—V.F. Gunaratna

We human beings don't like to think about death. The topic is far too depressing; way too dark.

So, why do Buddhists like to make us think about death? They're so committed to thinking about death and dying that a part of Buddhist monastic training is to spend a night of meditation in a cemetery.

And why does a Buddhist teacher say that "it is by understanding death that we understand life"?

One way to think about death that can help us understand life is to simply consider this thought: I could have died last night.

Many people die in the night. They die from a heart attack, an automobile accident, illness, suicide, murder. To deepen your appreciation of the new day, you could further consider that many other people on the planet died last night; that death has happened to men and women, young and old, babies and teenagers.

Understanding this, every morning when we wake up our first thought should be that of gratitude: How marvelous that I am still alive. How wonderful that I am receiving the gift of one more day. In fact, when we wake up every morning it is perfectly appropriate to remind ourselves: How glorious that I'm alive. I really could have died last night but here I am!

Thinking this way about death is a powerful reminder that life is fragile. Thinking this way about death is also a powerful reminder that every new day is a gift with endless possibilities for spiritual expansion and evolution.

DAY 100

Mid-Life Crisis or Kundalini Moment?

*There's more to us than the sniveling, snarling
organism that craves power and approval. The
clarity and contentment we seek lies deep inside us all.*
—Fortune Magazine Editorial

We all know people who make a major change in their lives. Usually this takes place around age forty. But it can take place earlier or later. The change often alarms both the person and those around them because it appears "drastic" and creates discomfort. It's often called a "mid-life crisis."

There is, however, another way to view such a change, one which is more positive and respectful. A term that relates to that perspective is *kundalini*, a Sanskrit word which literally means "coil." Kundalini is located at the base of the spine where it is said to be coiled three-and-half times. It is a powerful energy which can be aroused into action, affecting and altering one's consciousness. Kundalini is frequently mentioned in ancient Eastern texts as a coiled snake waiting to be awakened and ready to strike. Though it is present in every person, most are unaware of its existence. Only those who are mindful discover and tap into this power.

Interestingly, Eastern philosophy teaches that kundalini arises naturally in a person around age forty or so. In Western thought this emergence is erroneously and negatively described as a "mid-life crisis." However, Eastern thought understands this pattern positively, teaching that an awakened kundalini is expressed in a person who begins to see life differently, wishes to experience him- or herself in a fresh way and experiences a new energy and vigor which was previously latent and seemingly absent. It is a powerful time of self-realization and should be viewed most mindfully.

So, if you are making changes and transitions in your life, be encouraged, be mindful and be empowered. It may be your kundalini rising. Rather than judge it, remain curious and open. Kundalini rising is something which should be honored, respected and acted upon.

DAY 101

Parable of the Four Cups

When we are distracted, unwilling to learn, or preoccupied with other matters, it is not possible to receive the teachings.
—Tashi Nyima

Sadly, some people—perhaps too many—simply "fail to launch." Though opportunities are present and ample, they never emerge and evolve into their higher Self. Buddhism offers an explanation for this through a parable of four cups representing four types of personalities.

1. *The full cup.* When a cup is full, nothing more can be added. This applies to people who have "all the answers," who are full of their own ideas and concepts. There is no room for truth or new insights in a cup that is full. Keep the cup of your mind empty and open.
2. *The dirty cup.* When a cup is soiled, dirty or contains some toxic substance it will contaminate everything that is poured into it. These are people whose minds contain prejudice, discrimination, judgmentalism, faulty assumptions. They become arrogant and are unable to

learn and hold noble thoughts. Keep the cup of your mind clean, free of toxins.

3. *The inverted cup.* When a cup is inverted, nothing can get in, nothing can be contained. Think of people whose minds are made up; people whose belief system says, "my religion is the only truth." Keep the cup of your mind free from such illusions and delusions.

4. *The cracked cup.* When a cup is cracked you can still pour tea or water into it. However, the liquid will seep out and not be retained. These are people who may have good intentions, but they become careless, neglectful, scattered and are unable to follow through on commitments. Keep the cup of your mind free from becoming cracked by maintaining focus and discipline.

DAY 102

Everyone Has Eighty-Three Problems

The basic problem, actually, is how to get rid of the idea that we're going to get rid of our problems. Only then can we relate directly with the real issues of our life.
—Roshi Bernie Glassman

One of the most popular stories about the Buddha involves a man who came to consult with him. The man heard that the Buddha was not only a powerful spiritual teacher but a gifted counselor. So, he came asking for help with his many problems.

The man explained that he owned a large farm and that farming was a very risky endeavor. "Some years the crops are very good, but other years the rains don't come and my family nearly starves to death. Farming is a great source of worry for me," he said. Continuing on, the farmer added that he was married, that his wife was a "good woman but sometimes I find her very, very irritating." On top of that, the farmer said he had several children "all of whom are spoiled, refuse to work hard maintaining the farm and are often disrespectful to me." The man outlined a long litany of problems finishing with the statement, "I am a very unhappy man."

When he was through, the Buddha looked directly into the farmer's eyes and said: "I am sorry, but I cannot help you." Astonished and disappointed, the man said, "What do you mean? You're the Buddha but you can't help me?"

The Buddha elaborated saying: "Look, everybody has problems. In fact, every person has eighty-three problems and there's really nothing that can be done about that. If you solve one problem, there is always another problem right behind it." To drive his point home, the Buddha added: "Eventually, people you love are going to die and, see, that is a problem and there is nothing I can do about it. Furthermore, you are going to die and, see, that is a big problem and there is nothing I can do about it."

Now the man was not merely disappointed but angry. "You're supposed to be this great teacher and you are telling me you can't help me with my problems!" he shouted.

With this, the Buddha paused and said: "Well, I can't help you with the eighty-three problems, but I believe I can help you with your eighty-fourth problem." Puzzled, the man said, "eighty-fourth problem? What is the eighty-fourth problem?"

Said the Buddha: "That you don't want to have any problems."

The Buddha was trying to show the man that it's impossible to have life the way we want it at all times. Rather than trying to control, manipulate or fix life, we need to adjust ourselves to reality and deal with life on its terms. When unpleasant, unwelcome events and issues come our way, we need to avoid wasting energy being angry, frustrated and disappointed. Instead, we need to use our energies to respond creatively and courageously to those times.

DAY 103

Inner Versus Outer Success

While prosperity is in some ways related to money, it is not caused by money.
—Shakti Gawain

So many of my younger friends are eager for material success. They want to study only in areas that will bring them good jobs and big financial rewards. While there's nothing wrong with having a good job that pays well, it's not the only measurement for life success. Here's a simple exercise to use when you're feeling locked into the material aspect of life.

Recall some people you know who have achieved the very material successes you seek and ask yourself:

- Are they really any happier than I am?
- Are they experiencing more friendship and love in their lives than I do?
- Is greater peace of mind the result of their success?
- Are they kind, gentle, respectful toward others, or somewhat arrogant and rude?
- Does their lifestyle encourage them to engage in enlightenment-oriented practices?

Remind yourself that it is inner success that brings joy, tranquility, balance and peace of mind. And remember that, in our culture, success and excess come together in ways that are fulfillment-denying rather that fulfilling.

DAY 104

The Power of a Spiritual Friend

Critical to our spiritual progress is our selection of friends and companions.
—Victor M. Parachin

A young monk named Meghiya was the Buddha's personal assistant. One day when his duties were done, he decided to spend his free time in meditation at a nearby field. It was a beautiful and peaceful mango grove, an ideal place to sit quietly and meditate. However, as Meghiya sat there, his mind was restless and agitated. None of the techniques he knew seemed to give him the ability to manage his wandering, unfocused mind. This began to aggravate him and bring up angry feelings about meditation and about himself.

So, he stopped meditating and sought out the Buddha, explaining what had just happened. The Buddha used Meghiya's experience to stress an important teaching. "Meghiya," he said, "there are five conditions which create a calm and centered, strong and stable mind." Then he outlined them:

1. a spiritual friend
2. virtuous conduct
3. enlightened conversation

4. energy and enthusiasm
5. insight into life's impermanence.

The Buddha also said that the development of the last four were dependent upon the first point. So, to solidify this teaching, the Buddha re-explained it this way: "When you have a spiritual friend, there is virtuous conduct. When you have a spiritual friend, there is enlightened conversation. When you have a spiritual friend, there is energy and enthusiasm. And when you have a spiritual friend, you will have insight into life's impermanence."

It's commonly thought that being Buddhist means closeting oneself in a room and spending time in private, solitary meditation. While this is helpful, it is more important to develop spiritual friendships with like-minded people. That means gathering with others for meditation, chanting, teachings, retreats, study, service projects, etc. In Buddhism, going it alone means going nowhere. We need to have spiritual companions to accompany us on our journey.

DAY 105

Respecting All Lives

If one is the son of a Buddha, one must, with a merciful heart, practice the liberation of living beings... and cause others to do so.
—Brahmajala Sutra

One major difference between Buddhism and the three Western religions (Judaism, Islam and Christianity) is in the arena of compassion and kindness. Where the three Western religions stress love for one's fellow human beings, Buddhism expands love, kindness and compassion beyond just human beings toward all sentient beings—including humans, animals, fishes, and the nations of insects.

Therefore, it is no surprise that Buddhism vigorously promotes a vegetarian diet. Non-harming and non-killing means consideration for animal lives. Of course, one can follow a Buddhist path and still consume flesh foods, but the teachings of the Buddha will always point in the direction of vegetarianism. Throughout Buddhist history there have been outstanding times when compassion toward sentient beings was especially promoted. Here are some examples:

- The highly influential Indian Buddhist Emperor of India, Ashoka (268-223 BCE), said: "I have

enforced the law against killing animals ...but the greatest progress of righteousness among men comes from the exhortation in favor of non-injury to life and abstention from killing living beings."
- In ancient Japan, at a time when Buddhism was dominant, animal liberation was decreed by the emperors. Temmu, an emperor in the seventh century, issued an order of liberation in the year 676, "that all living beings be let loose." This included criminals not convicted of a capital crime as well as animals.
- In the year 745, also in Japan, Emperor Shomu ordered that all falcons and cormorants (birds trained to catch fish for humans) be set free. He also prohibited hunting and fishing using these birds.
- These Buddhist practices of liberation of animals also flourished in ancient China. Chinese emperor Hsu-tsung of the T'ang dynasty (618-906) dedicated eighty-one ponds for the liberation of living beings.
- Also in China, in the year 1032, a well-known Buddhist monk called "the Cloud of Compassion" made a huge pond for the liberation of living beings. Then, he held a special festival on the Buddha's birthday in the early spring, invited all the people of the district to

- participate, instructing them to let loose fish and birds into and around the pond.
- Up until the Chinese Communist revolution of 1949, near the main gate of every major Buddhist monastery there was a sizable pool for the release of fish that devotees had purchased and rescued from fish-sellers. Behind the monasteries, there were usually stables for the care of cows, pigs and other livestock similarly rescued.

Today, perhaps, you could consider how you can practice the "liberation of all living beings," especially with our animal companions on the planet.

DAY 106

Mistaken About Reality

We do not see things as they are, we see them as we are.
—Jewish Talmud

Buddhist teacher Steve Hagen tells a story from his youth when he and a friend did a cross-country road trip. At the time, Hagen owned a soft-top convertible. To save money, the two decided to camp as often as possible. Late one night, they arrived at a campground and set up a tent. They were both weary, so they retired promptly. Before getting into his sleeping bag, Hagen took of his watch and hung it on his car's turn signal. Since there were no other campers, he also put his wallet on the car dash. Then he crawled into his sleeping bag and fell asleep.

Before long, his companion woke him up. His friend had not camped before and was frightened by something moving around outside the tent. Hagen laughed it off, saying they should expect night animals to prowl around. Telling his friend there was nothing to worry about, he fell back asleep.

However, the next morning when he stepped out of the tent, he was shocked to see that the roof of his convertible had been slashed in a T-shape, allowing the sides of the roof to cave and creating a gaping hole.

Looking inside, he saw that his watch and his wallet were still there. It was simply an act of destruction not an act of theft. Hagen was extremely angry that someone would just slash the roof of his convertible for no reason except to damage his vehicle.

Later that morning, as he and his friends walked through the wood, they came upon a shredded box of cookies. There were no cookies left, just the remnants of the box. Hagen picked it up and threw it into the trash. When they were back at the car, his friend opened the glove compartment of Hagen's car and burst out: "Hey! My cookies are gone!" Right away, Hagen realized what had happened. His city friend was innocent enough to leave a box of cookies in the car overnight and a raccoon slashed the roof of his car in order to get those cookies.

Suddenly, Hagen's anger and bad feelings about the incident changed. When he thought someone had deliberately cut open his convertible roof, he was deeply disturbed and agitated. However, when he realized it was just a hungry raccoon foraging for food, he was no longer angry and no longer blaming. His mind was now at ease and relaxed.

It's important to note that the external circumstances had not changed: his beloved convertible vehicle had been seriously damaged. However, what did change was something internal within Hagen. His perception of the situation was altered such that there was no need or no place for feelings of anger and hostility. Sometimes, perception can be deception, preventing us from seeing events correctly. That's why, when we become upset about an issue, we need to pause, think and ask ourselves, "What's really going on here?"

DAY 107

A Mantra to Manage Road Rage

Sentient beings are equal in wanting happiness and not wanting suffering. They are equal in having a right to happiness and freedom from suffering.
—Jampa Tegchok

A contemporary Buddhist teacher tells of an incident that happened many years ago, when he was a young man. Driving to his parents' place one day, he became highly irritated by the very slow driver ahead of him. Angry, he tailgated the auto so closely that he couldn't even see the rear license plate on the vehicle ahead. His aggressive driving clearly intimidated the driver in front of him who seemed relieved by turning off onto a side road.

However, the side road was the very one he was taking to visit his parents. The driver was his own mother. Immediately, his rage turned to enormous shame and great guilt. Fortunately, he had the maturity and wisdom to learn from the experience and, from that time on, whenever he encountered a particularly slow driver or was cut off in traffic by a careless driver, he repeated this mantra to manage any road rage: "that could be my mother… that could be my mother … that could be my mother." That simple five-word phrase transformed hostility and anger into respect and love, impatience into acceptance.

The man's technique is a powerful one, which creates immediate consideration and compassion. So, the next time you are driving and become agitated by another driver, say to yourself "that could be my mother... or my father... or my sister or... my brother or... my boyfriend or... my girlfriend . . ."

DAY 108

Buddha's Final Instructions

There's a bright light of awareness that shines through each of us and guides us home, and we're never separated from this luminous awareness, any more than waves are separated from ocean.
—Tara Brach

It is believed that the Buddha died in his eighth decade. Anticipating death, his closest disciples asked him for a final teaching. These were his words: "Each of you be a light to yourself. Take to yourself no external refuge. Hold fast to the Truth. Look not for refuge to anyone beside yourself."

Unlike the majority of other religious leaders, who tell people to follow the teachings of a book, a teacher, or ecclesiastical authorities, the Buddha expresses complete confidence in humanity. You, yourself, are the final authority. You have within you everything that is needed to manage issues, direct your life, and forge pathways forward. You are your own light, your own authority. Do not become dependent upon a holy book, a priest, minister, rabbi, guru or your parents or your family. "Be a light to yourself" is the Buddha's final teaching. He reminds us that no community—politicians, governments, churches, parliaments, councils, philosophers, theologians—should be entrusted with the responsibility of the words, actions and directions our lives take.

Furthermore, the Buddha is saying that each one of us has all the power, wisdom, insight and courage necessary to deal with whatever issues and events come into our lives. And, this power is always present even when we feel hurt, lost, abandoned, discouraged or despairing. Of course, many people simply and quickly abdicate their personal responsibility giving personal authority to others and live by their instructions, teachings and directives. This is very "un-Buddhist."

Don't be seduced by other people and organizations that tell you they have the answers for your life issues. Be your own lamp; be your own light; be your own guru. The philosopher Krishnamurti wisely noted: "You cannot be a light to yourself if you are in the dark shadows of authority, of dogma, of conclusion."

Index

A
Abandon, Day 1
Adjust, Day 48
Aesop, Day 26
Ajahn Chah, Day 93
Akira Ishii, Day 97
Akiva, Rabbi, Day 87
Appearances, Day 73
Appreciate, Day 36
Attitude, Day 33, 69
Aurobindo, Day 82
Axworthy, Lloyd, Day 8

B
Bandit, Day 50
Batchelor, Stephen, Day 18
Benefiting others, Day 70
Bhagavad Gita, Day 24
Blame, Day 58
Bliss, Day 68
Blessings, Day 16
Boorstein, Sylvia, Day 67
Brach, Tara, Day 108
Brahmajala Sutra, Day 105
Braiker, Harriet, Day 38
Breathed, Berke, Day 41
Buddha, Day 1, 3, 18, 22, 30, 50, 51, 82, 85, 88, 92, 95, 96, 102, 108
Burroughs, John, Day 47
Buscaglia, Leo, Day 76

C
Calm, Day 61
Campbell, Joseph, Day 68
Chan Khong, Day 98
Change, Day 49, 77
Chodron, Pema, Day 35, 41
Churchill, Winston, Day 71
Clarity, Day 11
Cleansing, Day 85
Comparison, Day 31
Compassion, Day 78
Complain, Day 48
Contentment, Day 100
Cultivate, Day 2
Curiosity, Day 11, 20

D
Daisaku Ikeda, Day 61
Dalai Lama, Day 39, 69, 72, 76, 77
Death, Day 99
De Mestral, George, Day 11
DeSteno, David, Day 3
Devi, Indra, Day 89
Dhammananda, K., Day 81
Difficulty, Day 75

Disillusion, Day 32
Disquieting thoughts, Day 25
Divinity, Day 45
Doyle, Arthur Conan, Day 70

E
Eating mindfully, Day 98
Ego, Day 37
Emerson, Ralph Waldo, Day 29, 62
Einstein, Albert, Day 11
Enlightenment, Day 46, 79

F
Fear, Day 20
Fitting in, Day 24
Ford, Henry, Day 36
Four cups, Day 101
Four Noble Truths, Day 16
Franklin, Ben, Day 29
Friends, Day 52, 104
Funeral, Day 12

G
Generosity, Day 21, 64, 72
Gibran, Kahil, Day 33
Giving, Day 2
Glassman, Bernie, Day 102
Gratitude, Day 16
Gunartana, V. F, Day 99

Guru, Day 13

H
Habits, Day 60
Hafiz, Day 45
Hagen, Steve, Day 106
Halifax, Joan, Day 71
Hamsa bird, Day 43
Happiness, Day 41
Hawn, Goldie, Day 66
Heraclitus, Day 54
Heschel, Abraham J, Day 42
Hsing Yun, Day 50, 57
Hsuan Hua, Day 94

I
Impermanence, Day 54
Inner peace, Day 10
Ishi, Day 20
Ishin Yoshimoto, Day 97

J
Jampa Tegchok, Day 107
Jefferson, Thomas, Day 40
Jones, E. Stanley, Day 20
Journey, Day 65
Joy, Day 15
Judgment, Day 87

K
Karma, Day 84, 92
Kindness, Day 21, 39

King, Martin Luther Jr., Day 9, 53
Kundalini, Day 100

L
Lao Tzu, Day 65
LeShan, Lawrence, Day 55
Letting go, Day 56
Life, Day 92, 94, 95
Light, Day 53, 88, 108
Loss, Day 71
Love, Day 59

M
Maharishi Effect, Day 86
Maimonides, Day 9, 63
Mantra, Day 107
Materialism, Day 103
Matsumoto, Shoukei, Day 10
Mead, Margaret, Day 86
Meditation, Day 3, 35, 83, 95, 97
Meghiya, Day 104
Mid-life crisis, Day 100
Mind, Day 26, 30, 85, 89
Mindfulness, Day 51
Mithridates, Day 63
Moliere, Day 57
Morihei Ueshiba, Day 46

N
Negative, Day 74
Nhat Hanh, Thich, Day 4, 74, 83, 96, 98
Noble Eightfold Path, Day 4
Non-violence, Day 96, 105

O
Ogunlaru, Rasheed, Day 52
Olivier, Lawrence, Day 17
Optimism, Day 69

P
Patanjali, Day 25
Patience, Day 57
Peaceful, Day 41
Perfection, Day 17, 38
Pike, Albert, Day 72
Poison, 64
Positive thinking, Day 25
Practice, Day 91
Present moment, Day 67
Problems, Day 102
Progress, Day 38

Q
Questions, Day 19

R

Radhakrishnan, S., Day 51
Radmacher, Mary Anne, Day 73
Reacting, Day 14
Reality, Day 106
Red Pine, Day 6
Regrets, Day 90
Responding, Day 14
Rinchen, Sonam, Day 1
Road rage, Day 107
Roosevelt, Theodore, Day 31

S

Sai Weng, Day 54
Satchidananda, Swami, Day 60
Schweitzer, Albert, Day 27
Self-care, Day 55
Shantideva, Day 14, 63
Shakespeare, William, Day 56
Shakti Gawain, Day 103
Sheng Yen, Day 79
Shoukei Matsumoto, Day 10
Shusruta, Day 49
Silence, Day 5
Singletary, Michelle, Day 64
Sivananda, Swami, Day 74
Six accomplishments, Day 42
Snake, Day 58
Sorensen, Alfred Emmanuel, Day 5
Speech, Day 44
Spiritual, Day 27
Spiritual friends, Day 52, 104
Surya Das, Lama, Day 80
Suzuki, Shunryu, Day 48

T

Tagore Rabindranath, Day 5
Talmud, Day 106
Tashi Nyima, Day 101
Tetsugen Doko, Day 91
Thanissaro Bhikkhu, Day 28, 44
Therapy, Day 97
Thief, Day 62
Three Jewels, Day 6
Thoughts, Day 26
Tirukural, Day 52
Today, Day 34
Tolerance, Day 81
Tolle, Eckhart, Day 5
Trevelyan, G. M. Day 40
Touch, Day 76
Traleg Kyabgon, Day 75

Truman, Harry, Day 7
Trungpa, Chogyam, Day 60, 75
Tulku Thondup, Day 84

U
Unemployment, Day 7
Unitas, Johnny, Day 37

V
Vegetarian, Day 105
Virtue, Day 29

W
Walshe, Maurice, Day 12
War, Day 97

Wilde, Oscar, Day 16
Wisdom, Day 80
Witness, Day 92
Words, Day 44
Work, Day 8

Y
Yoga, Day 27, 95
Yin Shun, Day 2

Z
Zen, Day 15,
Zen Master, Day 66

Contact Information

ABOUT THE AUTHOR

VICTOR M. PARACHIN, M. DIV., is Director of the Tulsa Yoga Meditation Center and is a certified ayurvedic wellness consultant, meditation teacher and Yoga instructor. He is the author of a dozen books about both Eastern and Western spiritual practices, including *Eastern Wisdom for Western Minds* (Orbis Books), *Healing Grief* (Chalice Press), and *Daily Strength for Daily Needs* (Ligouri Press). He is a graduate from the University of Toronto School of Theology. Parachin has maintained a personal meditation practice for nearly thirty years, long before meditation and mindfulness became part of the popular vocabulary. He is a full-time freelance journalist and author, and conducts retreats and workshop regularly. He lives in Tulsa, Oklahoma.

Website: tulsayogameditationcenter.com

ABOUT HOHM PRESS

HOHM PRESS is committed to publishing books that provide readers with alternatives to the materialistic values of the current culture, and promote self-awareness, the recognition of interdependence, and compassion. Our subject areas include parenting, transpersonal psychology, religious studies, women's studies, the arts and poetry.

Contact Information: Hohm Press, PO Box 4410, Chino Valley, Arizona, 86323, USA; 800-381-2700, or 928-636-3331; email: publisher@hohmpress.com

Visit our website: www.hohmpress.com